"This is an important book for anyone involved in the planning and execution of the Paschal Triduum. It is highly accessible, easy to read, and filled with many helpful details that are both pastoral in their perspective and liturgical in their grounding. Helmes knows the tradition, the theology, and the practice. Coupled with his wealth of experience, this book has the potential to educate and inspire both liturgical ministers and the entire assembly. Highly recommended!"

—Judith M. Kubicki, CSSF
Associate Professor of Theology
Fordham University

"If you are looking for an informative, practical, organized book to assist pastors, deacons, musicians, worship commissions, and art and environment committees prepare for the Sacred Triduum liturgies, *Three Great Days: Preparing the Liturgies of the Paschal Triduum* is a must-have resource. Jeremy Helmes, a musician, liturgist, and seasoned parish minister, systematically walks through the celebration of the Paschal Triduum: its history, the liturgies, personnel needs, checklists, tips for liturgical ministers, a timeline, and much more. Jeremy's academic study and years of parish experience has enabled him to provide informed, practical recommendations and ideas, as well as useful tips which will assist any liturgy committee as they prepare for the Triduum. Also, don't miss the several appendices, which are of great value in and of themselves. To ensure a well-prepared and well-celebrated Triduum, *Three Great Days* will surely help you in this endeavor!"

—Karen Kane
Director of Worship
Archdiocese of Cincinnati

THREE GREAT DAYS

PREPARING THE LITURGIES OF THE PASCHAL TRIDUUM

JEREMY HELMES

LITURGICAL PRESS
Collegeville, Minnesota

www.litpress.org

Library of Congress Cataloging-in-Publication Data

Names: Helmes, Jeremy A. (Jeremy Andrew), 1979– author.
Title: Three great days : preparing the liturgies of the Paschal triduum / Jeremy Helmes.
Description: Collegeville : Liturgical Press, 2016.
Identifiers: LCCN 2016018145 | ISBN 9780814646021 (pbk.)
Subjects: LCSH: Paschal triduum—Liturgy. | Catholic Church—Liturgy.
Classification: LCC BX2015.785 .H45 2016 | DDC 264/.02—dc23
LC record available at https://lccn.loc.gov/2016018145

To the faith communities with whom I have worshiped and ministered for the Paschal Triduum: St. Vivian, St. Anthony, St. John Neumann, St. Bartholomew, the University of Dayton, and St. Maximilian Kolbe. To their leaders, ministers, and members: thank you for helping me grow in love for the three great days through your intense and passionate celebration of the dying and rising Christ.

Contents

CONTENTS

PREFACE

How to Use This Book

As a means for preparing parish liturgies for the Paschal Triduum, this book is intended as a resource both for those who are undertaking this preparation process for the first time and for those veterans who want a fresh take on things, or reminders of important details. You should be able to consult it each year (perhaps on your first day back to work after Christmas break!) as a way to kick off your Triduum preparation process.

After two chapters on the "why," "what," and "who," you'll find a chapter on each of the principal liturgies, which includes an outline of the rite, some liturgical theology and history, general information, and a "walkthrough" of the liturgy. Included are some "tips" for various ministry categories (e.g., music ministers, presiders, etc.). Even if those ministers don't read this whole book, you (or the preparation team leader) can make sure all the ministers consider creative ideas by inviting them to peruse the tips in these chapters.

Chapter 7 looks at other liturgies during the Triduum, such as Liturgy of the Hours, Way of the Cross, and other devotions. Finally, the appendices include some sample texts for use when the Roman Missal suggests things are said, but provides no text.

Once you've assembled your preparation team and all those involved know their responsibilities, it's time to establish a timeline and the important tasks to be accomplished. You'll find a detailed timeline in the appendices; adapt it and make it your own.

Note that you should be thinking during *this* year's Triduum about how to make *next* year's liturgies even better. Make notes, ask others for feedback, keep track of ideas you have for the future. You don't have to "solve" every problem now: just take note of something you'd like to "fix" next year, and then as you approach the immediate preparation period (winter), the team can look at solutions. Use the evaluation tool in the appendices to reflect on what was good this year and what you can do better next year.

Later on, as we look carefully at each of the principal liturgies, you'll also want to consult the appendices, which include a detailed setup/to-do list of preparations for each day of the Triduum. As with the timeline, adapt these checklists to make them your own, and revisit them each year, keeping them accurate.

Year after year, as you prepare for the most important liturgical season, this book will provide you with guidance to enable you and your faith community to celebrate the Paschal Triduum with joy.

ACKNOWLEDGMENTS

This project began as a collection of resources I had developed over the years of preparing parish liturgies for the Paschal Triduum. Thanks to Barry Hudock and everyone at Liturgical Press for the invitation to prepare this book as an aid to faith communities who want to prepare and celebrate well the holiest days of our liturgical year.

I am grateful to so many people whose support and assistance made this book possible. First, to my wife, Karen, for picking up some "extra slack" with our children while I clicked and clacked in the other room.

Thanks to the many colleagues, pastoral ministers, and parish worship leaders with whom I've had the opportunity to collaborate on the Paschal Triduum over the years: Fr. Len Wenke, Sr. Jeannie Masterson, Pat Bergen, Fr. Bill Farris, Sr. Janet Schneider, Jim Pera, Fr. Jerry Chinchar, SM, Carol Heuser, and so many others. Many of the ideas contained in this book are a result of our collaboration, with much trial and error!

Thanks to my colleagues and fellow pastoral ministers who reviewed the manuscripts and offered feedback: Karen Kane, Sarah Merkel, Mary Ella Wielgos, Deacon Mike Lippman, Tim McManus, and Fr. Steve Walter. I'm especially grateful to my friend and colleague Emily Strand, who offered her experience as an author and liturgical minister in critique of this text, her time in reading and responding, and her shared conviction that the paschal mystery is what it's all about!

Thanks to the people of St. Maximilian Kolbe Parish in Cincinnati, Ohio, for whom I have been privileged to serve as liturgist and musician for the past six years, alongside my good friend and their pastor, Fr. Geoff Drew. Inspired by the sacrifice of their patron, the people of St. Max truly delight in the opportunity each year to celebrate the source and summit of our liturgical year.

I'm so thankful for all the assistance offered in preparing this book. Of course, the opinions and errors in the book are mine alone.

Standing meekly in the shadows of many fine scholars and authors on the Triduum—giants such as Gabe Huck, Paul Turner, Lawrence Johnson, Michael Joncas, and many others—I hope that this book will offer some assistance to anyone who now shoulders the joyous burden of preparing parish liturgies for these three great days.

1

WHAT'S SO "GREAT" ABOUT THESE THREE DAYS?

"First things first!" "They broke the mold after that one!" "Let's start at the very beginning." "Begin with the end in mind." These expressions remind us that first things are very important. Laying a good foundation, starting off right: these are important for the success of any endeavor.

My wife is a pharmacist so I pay attention to news from the prescription drug industry. I'm fascinated (and a bit dismayed) by the outrageously high cost of medicine these days in our country, but I understand a bit about how it works. In reality, the costs of expensive prescription medication aren't the same for each pill: typically, each pill made costs only a fraction of a cent to manufacture, but the first one costs hundreds of millions of dollars. The most expensive part of making prescription drugs is up front: the drug companies spend all the money up front to get things right—research, development, trials, testing, retesting, evaluating, preparing for production, making sure they have everything figured out before they go on to produce millions of potentially life-saving pills. It makes more sense to spend money and time beforehand to make sure the first pill is right, because all the other pills they make afterward will benefit from the important work put into the first one. Thorough preparation for the most important pill—the first one—is key to making effective prescription medication.

I couldn't help but think about this when reflecting upon the importance of the Paschal Triduum in the context of the whole liturgical year. Since the Triduum is the most important season, the high point of the calendar, it deserves the most attention, the most time, the most energy, and the most preparation. When we prepare well for these important days, the remainder of the liturgical year will benefit from our hard work. Parishes that "get the Triduum right" reap the benefits for 362 days to follow!

Whether it means the fullest use of sacred symbols, the best processions, art, and environment that really inspires and stirs the heart, or music that truly moves us and helps us express our faith, the Paschal Triduum has the capacity to set the tone for the balance of the liturgical calendar.

The word *triduum* comes from the Latin for "three days." Adding the word *paschal* makes it clear that these three days are about the dying and rising of Jesus Christ, what we call the "paschal mystery." "In the Sacred Triduum, the Church solemnly celebrates the greatest mysteries of our redemption" (Roman Missal, Sacred Paschal Triduum 1).

How did this three-day festival come to be the center of the entire liturgical year? Why does it matter?

From Passover to Pascha:
A Brief History of the Paschal Triduum

Sunday has always been known as "the Lord's Day": the first day of the week, the day of the sun, the day of the church, and the day of the resurrection. The earliest followers of Jesus gathered each and every Sunday as a community to remember and celebrate their friend and teacher in the sharing of sacred stories and the breaking of the bread. To this day, the Sunday Eucharist continues as the church's weekly celebration of the dying and rising of Christ.

The first disciples, as devout Jews, also continued to celebrate many of the feasts of their Jewish heritage. An important annual feast was that of Passover, the spring commemoration of how God saved the chosen people and delivered them from the clutches of the pharaoh. In the annual Passover celebration, the Jewish people feasted upon a roasted lamb, sacrificed in remembrance of the lamb's blood sprinkled upon the doorposts of the Israelites. Passover celebrated both God's "passing over" and sparing the lives of the firstborn sons of the chosen people and the Israelites "passing over" from the slavery in Egypt to freedom.

The first Christians saw in Jesus Christ the new Lamb of God, sacrificed anew for the sake of God's people. They saw Jesus' own death as a new Passover: Jesus "passed over" from death to new life. Jesus' last meal with his friends was almost assuredly a Passover meal. The disciples understood that Jesus of Nazareth was the fulfillment of God's promise to the people of Israel, and that Jesus' own Passover was to be remembered and celebrated in the new Christian community.

Thus the feast of *Pascha* (the Greek term, derived from the Hebrew *Pesach*) was born as an annual feast for the Christian community, celebrated in conjunction with the traditional feast of Passover. In many ways it became—and remains—a "big Sunday," the annual festival of Christ's triumph over death. The early Christian community began to anticipate its celebration with an all-night vigil leading up to the celebration itself. Liturgical practices varied widely in that time, but we know that it typically included a service of Scriptures, including readings and psalms, and a eucharistic celebration. Over time, the vigil began to include the baptism of new Christians.

As the church matured and grew, other liturgies developed on the days prior to the Paschal Vigil and Sunday to commemorate the final events of Jesus' life. Thursday and Friday saw liturgical services to recall and celebrate the Last Supper and the Passion. Over time three days were observed as one unit, a *triduum*. Throughout history the precise beginning and ending of the Triduum has varied, with the modern definition being from the beginning of the Mass of the Lord's Supper on Holy Thursday night until sundown—after Vespers—on Easter Sunday.

The way in which the liturgies of the Paschal Triduum have been celebrated has varied greatly throughout history. Elements have been added and removed. Times for the principal liturgies have moved around based on the emphases of the era. At a low point prior to the reforms of 1955, the Easter Vigil—imbued with texts and imagery of light piercing darkness—was celebrated on Holy Saturday morning, in full daylight. It had become mostly a clerical affair, with most of the faithful uninterested or perhaps even uninvited! Holy Thursday's Mass of the Lord's Supper was also sparsely attended. The Triduum was not experienced as the early Christians envisioned it, a high point of the year. It was, at best, a relief from Lent, and a prelude to Easter Sunday.

We can see this attitude toward the Paschal Triduum reflected in the 1947 liturgical document *Mediator Dei*. As scholar Patrick Regan points out in his book *Advent to Pentecost* (Liturgical Press, 2012), the focus prior to the 1955 reforms was almost exclusively on the Passion of Christ, with little attention to the Resurrection of Christ (155). *Mediator Dei* describes it thus: "In Holy Week, when the most bitter sufferings of Jesus Christ are put before us by the liturgy, the Church invites us to come to Calvary and follow in the blood-stained footsteps of the divine Redeemer, to carry the cross willingly with Him, to reproduce in our own hearts His spirit of expiation and atonement, and to die together with Him" (158).

As Regan notes, the prevailing understanding in the first half of the twentieth century was a sharp separation between Holy Week (as the end of Lent) and the beginning of Eastertide: the ancient conception of a *triduum* of days as a "hinge" between the two would not be restored until the coming reforms. Prior to the reforms enacted by Pope Pius XII and the Second Vatican Council, Christ's death and Resurrection were celebrated sequentially: one during Holy Week, one during Eastertide.

In 1955, significant reforms to the Triduum (in fact, all of Holy Week) were enacted by Rome, due in part to the liturgical movement of the twentieth century. These reforms were codified after the Second Vatican Council in the 1970 Roman Missal, and largely constitute the modern celebration of these three great days.

The Triduum was restored to preeminence in the liturgical year, and all the liturgical documents now make clear that it celebrates not only the Passion and death of Jesus but also his Resurrection. These three days were now more precisely called the Sacred *Paschal* Triduum. The 1969 *Universal Norms on the Liturgical Year and the Calendar* now makes it clear that the Sacred Paschal Triduum is a distinct season from both Lent and Eastertide, and accords the Triduum the highest rank of all liturgical time.

What is it that makes these days so great? How does the liturgical festival called Triduum unfold? How is the paschal mystery celebrated during this brief season in a way like no other?

In Marty Haugen's liturgical song "We Remember," the liturgical action of the church is described as threefold: we *remember*, we *celebrate*, we *believe*. The Paschal Triduum, as the liturgical event *par excellence*, embodies this paradigm.

We Remember

All liturgy is about remembering: we remember how God has loved us throughout all times, from the very dawn of creation. In the liturgy, we participate in a kind of "holy remembering" called *anamnesis*, in which the past becomes present through our recollection. At no time during the liturgical year is this more palpable than during the Paschal Triduum, aided by the powerful symbols and sacred signs, dramatic narratives of salvation history, and rituals of our ancestors.

When we remember the history of our salvation, God's saving love is made real in our midst; in the Eucharist past and future become present at the foot of the cross. More than any other time in the liturgical year, the liturgies of the Paschal Triduum invite us to remember *who* we are and *whose* we are.

We Celebrate

Of course mere remembering is never enough. Holy remembering leads to celebration, the enactment of sacred ritual. During these three great days, the church celebrates a multitude of rituals, passed down to us through the centuries, many of which are celebrated only once each year. Some have historical significance attached to the liturgical day (like the adoration of the cross on Good Friday). Others, like the washing of feet on Holy Thursday, are so closely united to the institution of the Eucharist and the ministerial priesthood, which we commemorate on Holy Thursday.

More than any other time during the entire year, the Christian community ritualizes its paschal faith during the Triduum. In procession, by firelight, with rich and abundant symbols, in song ancient and new, with splendor and simplicity, the church celebrates the dying and rising of Jesus Christ.

We Believe

The ancient liturgical maxim *lex orandi, lex credendi* rings most true during the Paschal Triduum. The law of prayer is the law of belief: how we pray shapes our belief. Rather than simply bringing the catechism to life through sacred drama, the liturgy brings together the children of God as the Body of Christ, and we experience Christ truly present in our midst. Our faith is not only derived from, but confirmed by, the celebration of the liturgy.

In remembering and celebrating the salvation won for us by Jesus, we are confirmed and strengthened in our faith. Far from mere novelty or spectacle, the liturgies of these three great days manifest our belief in the power of God to conquer death. When we light the new fire and the paschal candle pierces the darkness of Holy Saturday night, our faith in Jesus, the Light of the World, is renewed. When we approach the cross on Good Friday and venerate it with a kiss, our belief in God's unending love is rekindled. When we are sprinkled with blessed baptismal water at the Easter Vigil or on Easter Sunday, we show forth our deepest belief that just as water has the power to cleanse and renew, the dying and rising of Christ—in which our baptism makes us sharers—both cleanses us and renews us!

A Twofold Obligation

The obligation for us to participate each Sunday in Mass is no secret to anyone: it's one of the hallmarks of being a Catholic Christian. There are some other non-Sunday feasts during the liturgical year on which the faithful have an obligation to participate in Mass: the Nativity of the Lord (Christmas Day), the solemnities of the Assumption and Immaculate Conception of Mary, the solemnity of Mary, the Mother of God, and the solemnity of All Saints. These vary from region to region, and diocese to diocese, throughout the world, but in every place, there are a few days each year, in addition to Sunday, on which we're expected to celebrate the Eucharist because they are so important to our life as Catholic Christians.

Why, then, are the days of the Paschal Triduum not all holy days of obligation? Other than Easter Sunday (like any other Sunday), there is no obligation for the faithful to participate in any aspects of the Triduum. Even though the church, in the *Universal Norms on the Liturgical Year and the Calendar*, ranks the days of the Triduum as the "high point of the entire liturgical year," these are not days of obligation (18).

A pastor friend of mine, confronted with this truth and in need of encouraging words for his flock about participating in the Triduum, explained it very simply. Celebrating Jesus' dying and rising for our salvation during the Paschal Triduum is not merely about obligation. Obligation is relatively easy. Participating in the Paschal Triduum is about *love*: certainly the love God showed for us hanging on the cross, but also our love for God. Love is much harder than obligation: it requires more from us, and the stakes are higher.

Consider spouses who show affection for one another. There is no obligation for a husband to kiss his wife at the start or end of the day—their vows didn't specify this! Yet it is out of love that spouses show each other affection, and all the other sacrifices and gestures that people in love do for one another.

Love is the reason why we celebrate the Paschal Triduum, and what should compel the faithful to join in the celebrations. Pastoral leaders should help people grow from understanding the role of liturgy as merely fulfilling one's obligation to an understanding of liturgy as expression of love for God. In fact, the Roman Missal itself exhorts this kind of pastoral leadership: "Pastors should, therefore, not fail to explain to the Christian faithful, as best they can, the meaning and order of the celebrations and to prepare them for active and fruitful participation" (Roman Missal, Sacred Paschal Triduum 2).

The second obligation is of the parish community to prepare well for these most important days. There are many important priorities for the parish liturgical leaders during the winter and spring: preparations for first penance, First Communion, confirmation, the weekly grind of preparing each Sunday, Lenten Way of the Cross and penance services, and more. It's hard to make time to prepare the Triduum liturgies with so many other pressing concerns. Relative to Palm and Easter Sundays—which are typically the most well attended of all fifty-two—the principal liturgies of the Triduum generally aren't the most popular. If we want to spend our time, energy, and resources on the liturgies with the most people, Holy Thursday, Good Friday, and the Easter Vigil will not make the cut.

The challenge here is not just to focus on the liturgies that are popular and bring the most people, but rather to focus on the liturgies that celebrate the most important facets of our faith. Jesus was rarely interested in what was popular, and was perfectly content with a gathering of only a few: what mattered was bringing people back to God and the Gospel message of God's great love for us.

You're probably already convinced of the importance of celebrating well and preparing thoroughly the Paschal Triduum liturgies because you're reading this book! It will be important for you, then, to encourage your colleagues, your parishioners, and anyone who's not yet bought in to the notion that these three days are worth the effort. These liturgies celebrate the core mysteries of our faith. These three days set the tone for the rest of the year. Get the preparation right; invest the time and energy and your parish will benefit throughout the whole year.

2

GETTING STARTED
AND ENGAGING
THE PARISH COMMUNITY

So, you're ready to begin preparing for the Paschal Triduum . . . what's first? How do you tackle the preparation for these complicated, richly symbolic, lengthy liturgies, densely packed into three days? Two things are clear: first, it takes the whole community. The entire parish, especially the parish leadership, must see the preparation of the Triduum liturgies as a priority for the whole parish. This chapter will explore the ways in which everyone in the parish can get involved, and the important duties of key people.

Second, start early. Your remote preparation for the Triduum should begin as soon after Christmas as you can get your brain working again! This chapter will help you develop a timeline that will make preparation manageable.

Roles and Responsibilities

A Leadership Team

Any project of this scope requires a team of leaders to see it to completion. This leadership team should be comprised of between three and nine key people, depending on the particular dynamics and personnel (staff and parishioners) in your parish. Below, I've outlined the specific responsibilities of some of these people in the preparation process. Forming some of them into a leadership team will keep everyone rowing the boat in the same direction.

If you have a staff member or key parishioner whose main responsibility is the liturgical life of the parish (like a director of worship or pastoral associate for liturgy), he or she would likely make the best team leader. This person will convene the leadership team, keep the team on track, facilitate discussions and decision making, communicate important details to other ministers, and keep the pastor apprised of the team's work. The team leader will make sure everyone follows the timeline and fulfills assigned tasks.

Other team members should be drawn from among those responsible for the various facets of the liturgy: music ministry leaders, art and environment coordinator, initiation minister(s), leaders of important liturgical ministries like lectors or altar servers. You might also consider a parish facilities manager or parish communications coordinator to be attached to the team somehow—even if this person doesn't meet regularly with the team, she or he should be informed of its work, and consulted about the areas of parish life in which she or he works.

In some situations, the pastor might be a working member of the preparation team, or even serve as the team leader, especially where staff and key parish leaders are limited or not available to serve. However, the pastor has his own role in the preparation process, and the work of leading the preparation team is best left to someone the pastor trusts and with whom he can stay in close contact.

We'll talk more about the duties of the leadership team later on when we review the timeline. For now, let's explore the roles and responsibilities of key people within the parish.

The Pastor

The pastor sets the liturgical tone for the parish. He has the responsibility to oversee the parish's worship, to make sure that parish liturgies are executed with reverence, style, and grace. The pastor is also the ultimate authority regarding what happens in parish life. Key decisions regarding the Paschal Triduum—especially those that involve new ideas or major changes from years past—will need his approval and support. The pastor should serve as a cheerleader for the preparation team and work to engage all the parish leaders, and parishioners themselves, in both preparation and celebration of these great days. Since he will likely preside for one or more of the principal liturgies, he will probably have some input on some of the liturgical details as well.

Other Priests (Presiders, Preachers, Concelebrants)

If more than one priest ministers in your parish, the liturgies of the Paschal Triduum may involve more than just one presiding priest. Even if the pastor presides for all the principal liturgies of Holy Thursday, Good Friday, and the Easter Vigil with other priests concelebrating, the liturgies of Easter Sunday morning may involve multiple presiders.

If you have more than one priest who will preside during your parish's Triduum, rather than consulting them for their personal preferences on the details of the Triduum liturgies, consider their talents and how they would best serve the parish at prayer. For example, while all three days could involve more presidential singing than normal, Good Friday—with its lengthy solemn intercessions and the Passion—would be a wonderful opportunity for a priest who sings well to preside.

If a priest other than the pastor is particularly involved in initiation ministry, consider involving him at least in the preparation for the Easter Vigil, or perhaps for the whole Triduum. Perhaps he might even serve as principal celebrant for the Easter Vigil, with the pastor concelebrating, or at least the assisting priest might preach for the Easter Vigil. Be careful, though, about assuming that just because Fr. John leads the RCIA that he should preside for the Easter Vigil, or even celebrate the liturgy of initiation. The Easter Vigil, while certainly the climax of the RCIA, is also a parish liturgy, and the preeminent one of the year at that, and so the pastor rightly has a role. If you have multiple priests participating in the Easter Vigil, choose your presiding minister and homilist with great care.

In consultation with the pastor, keep other priests who will preside and preach apprised of important liturgical details, especially where the rituals allow for options. When possible, consider involving them in decision making for the liturgies at which they will preside, while maintaining the continuity of the three days and all the liturgies together.

Master(s) of Ceremonies

For these complicated and unique liturgies, it might be helpful to assign one person to serve as a master of ceremonies for each of the principal liturgies, or for the whole Triduum. A good master of ceremonies serves to gently direct the ritual action, allowing the ministers to more fully enter into the rites and execute their duties gracefully.

This person might vest in an alb like the other lay ministers and actively assist them, directing them physically, facilitating movement and ritual from a place in the sanctuary like other ministers. This person might also simply be the "point person" for the liturgy behind the scenes, making sure that all the ministers are on the same page (figuratively and literally).

The MC for the liturgy need not make all the liturgical decisions, but should be the one who will rehearse other ministers as needed, think through the routes of processions, make sure all the materials, vessels, supplies are prepared and accessible.

If the preparation team leader will not be the MC for the liturgy, she should communicate clearly with the MC and the presiding priest so everyone knows how the liturgies are planned to unfold.

In spite of its grandiose title, the role of master of ceremonies is a humble, behind-the-scenes one, ensuring the liturgy unfolds with reverence and according to plan. Whoever the MC is, he or she must be well prepared, experienced in this role, familiar with the ritual books and rubrics of the

Triduum, trusted by both the preparation team and the presiding priest, familiar with the ministers involved, and able to be "invisible." Choose your MC(s) wisely!

Deacons

Like in other liturgies, all of the functions assigned to the deacon during the Paschal Triduum can be assumed by other ministers—concelebrating priest, lay minister (cantor, reader, etc.), or even the presiding priest himself. However, the liturgies of the Paschal Triduum include important and unique duties for the deacon, including the proclamation of the Passion, the solemn intercessions of Good Friday, bearing the paschal candle, the *Exsultet* proclamation of the Easter Vigil, and more. If deacons serve your parish, you'll need to make sure they are prepared for their duties.

No liturgy requires more than one deacon to minister, but there are opportunities for multiple deacons to serve. One such example would be the Easter Vigil, where one deacon might take the diaconal functions for the light ritual and Liturgy of the Word, while one deacon assumes the diaconal roles during the liturgies of initiation and Eucharist. If you are blessed with multiple deacons who all sing well, consider having a trio of deacons chant the Good Friday Passion.

It will be important for the deacon(s) to understand their roles (especially for the unique rituals not normally celebrated on a Sunday), to physically practice some of them (like carrying the cross on Good Friday or the paschal candle at the Easter Vigil), and to prepare for all the texts they will proclaim or sing. Don't underestimate how early in the preparation process to begin working with your deacon(s), especially if they have jobs outside the parish and other commitments.

Music Ministers

Of all the arts at the service of the liturgy, sacred music is of the highest priority. Sung prayer has the capacity to move and inspire us in ways that mere speech cannot. Those who lead the parish's music ministry should be involved in the preparation process, and ensure that music is well integrated in the Triduum liturgies. Like any Sunday, but especially during the Paschal Triduum, music isn't merely what we do while we wait for the next thing; rather music *is* an integral part of the rite. As we look carefully at each of the principal liturgies, we'll look at some important musical elements that should be considered during the preparation process.

As we consider music ministry during the Paschal Triduum, it's important to remember that these liturgies are for the whole parish. These liturgies should reflect the diversity of the parish—ethnically, stylistically, culturally. If your parish is fortunate enough to be served by multiple ensembles or choirs, start thinking now about how everyone can work together in service to the Triduum liturgies. Rather than assigning each liturgy to one ensemble or choir, consider involving all your ministers in all of the principal liturgies.

Also, it's important to think strategically about musical repertoire for the Paschal Triduum. How will you learn music for these unique, once-a-year rituals? How will your music ministers learn and lead so much music with limited rehearsal time? Consider ways to incorporate some of the music you know you will use during the Triduum at other times of the year, when you can learn it better, and lighten the burden of preparing so much all at the end of Lent. To make this possible, thorough evaluation after the previous year's Triduum will be essential (more on that in appendix D).

Art and Environment Team

Lasting only three days' time, the Paschal Triduum is the shortest season of the liturgical year. Yet it has the highest demands for liturgical decor. Complicating things further is the timeliness required by the transitions in liturgical decor: the utter starkness of Good Friday must give way rather quickly to the glorious splendor of Easter. The parish's art and environment ministers—those who manage the plants and flowers, candles, altar linens and other fabrics, banners, vestments, and other decorative items—should be key players in your Triduum preparation.

Art and environment ministers should start thinking early on about key questions: What should the design be for the new paschal candle? How will Holy Thursday look different from Lent and also different from Easter? How many hands will be needed to create beautiful decor for each of the days? These questions cannot be answered in a vacuum either; lilies could encircle the baptismal font, but there must be room for the elect to enter and exit during the liturgy of initiation. Where will the paschal candle be located? If the newly blessed sacred oils are included in procession on Holy Thursday, where will they come from, and where will they end up?

Initiation Ministers

The Easter Vigil is the culmination, the high point of the entire Rite of Christian Initiation of Adults. This liturgy is the annual celebration of baptism for adults and older children. The liturgy of initiation—the third of this four-part liturgy—is a complex sequence of rites governed by multiple ritual books, potentially involving many people. For this reason alone, those who coordinate Christian initiation in your parish should be part of the Triduum preparation process.

In addition to the great Vigil, the elect may take part in preparatory rites on Holy Saturday morning, participate in other principal liturgies (with or without their usual dismissal), and claim their rightful place in the liturgical assembly on Easter Sunday, clad in their white garment, still smelling of chrism! It will be helpful to have members of your initiation ministry collaborating on the preparation for the entire Triduum.

Ministry Coordinators

Just like a Sunday Mass in your parish, many lay liturgical ministers are needed to fulfill their roles with devotion and reverence. This will require careful preparation by both the ministers and the coordinators of the ministries. The Paschal Triduum also requires a large number of ministers, especially lectors, servers, and ministers of hospitality (ushers and greeters).

Not only do these liturgies differ significantly from a typical Sunday Mass in your parish—with which these lay ministers are most comfortable and familiar—but there are many options from which the preparation team will have to choose and notify those involved. Don't underestimate the complexity of moving large numbers of people in procession from a blazing bonfire outside the church, in total darkness, into a pitch-black church lit only by the paschal candle. Or the difficulty of proclaiming lengthy readings like the Passion, or the readings from Exodus and Isaiah for Holy Thursday and Good Friday, or the rich narratives during the Easter Vigil. Rather than being overwhelmed by larger-than-normal crowds on Easter Sunday morning, make sure your ministers of hospitality are well prepared to welcome all who come to celebrate the resurrection!

Other Parish Leaders

Because the liturgies of the Paschal Triduum are the high point of the liturgical year, and the liturgy is the heart of parish life, other key parish leaders should be involved in the preparation and celebration of these three days.

Make sure those who are responsible for parish communications are in the loop on important details. Unless your parish is the rare exception to the norm, these liturgies other than Easter Sunday are much less attended than Sunday Mass. A good communications plan, a "Paschal Triduum Marketing Strategy," for the parish can do wonders to increase participation by the whole parish. Consider not only your typical modes of communication (i.e., bulletin, website, social media) but also other modes like postcards, phone call campaigns, door-to-door invitations, and more.

In some cases, the Triduum liturgies include processions to or from places outside the main worship space. A bonfire for Easter Vigil might take place outside on the campus. The chapel of reservation for Holy Thursday night might not be in the church or the usual adoration chapel. Perhaps you need overflow seating or a simultaneous second Mass in a satellite location on campus for Easter Sunday. All of these will require some teamwork with those staffers and parishioners who manage the parish's facilities. Even simple things, like turning off parking lot lights for the beginning of the Easter Vigil or draining and refilling the immersion font for adult baptisms, will be easier if you include the facilities people in your preparation process.

Worship Commission

The proper role of the parish worship commission is to do what it normally does: to advise the pastor and key pastoral leaders about the worship life of the parish at the "macro" level. Rather than making decisions about liturgical details (which are best left to those who oversee ministers or have professional competence in the field), the worship commission should consider how the liturgies of the Triduum effectively invite the faithful into the celebration of the paschal mystery. Does our parish's celebration of the great three days truly enable us to manifest our faith in the dying and rising Christ?

The worship commission could be asked to consider some "big-picture" questions, especially those with a pastoral dimension. Does the number of readings for the Easter Vigil need to be reduced for any pastoral reason? Is our communications strategy for parishioners and others in the area working and reaching people? Will the musical texts chosen and the preaching enable the liturgical assembly to enter into prayer? The worship commission should play a special role in evaluating the liturgies from a pastoral perspective after the three days are completed. (See appendix D for a sample evaluation tool for the worship commission.) Resist the urge to bring detailed decisions before the worship commission; trust your leadership team and its members to make the detailed decisions, consulting the ritual books and their rubrics, in light of the parish and its people.

Other Parish Groups

Because there are some unique rituals as part of the Triduum liturgies, consider asking some parish groups to "manage" a particular part. For example, if you want to honor the rubric that the Easter Vigil begins with a blazing fire (*rogus ardens*), ask your parish's Boy Scout Troop to handle this. Not only will you benefit from a wonderful bonfire but you'll also involve several young people (and their families) in a liturgy they might not otherwise experience.

If you plan to adorn the church with flowers and light candles throughout the church during the Gloria of the Easter Vigil, consider asking last year's neophytes and their sponsors to carry pots in procession. If your *Mandatum* ritual of washing feet on Holy Thursday will involve more than twelve people, you'll need assistance with pitchers of water, bowls, and towels. Consider asking an existing parish group, like the youth ministry, to facilitate this ritual.

In all cases, explain how their assigned ritual fits in context of the liturgy, and of the three-day Triduum. Help them understand what needs to be done, and when, and how many people are needed. Then, watch as they take delight in serving the parish at prayer on these holy days.

3

HOLY THURSDAY
MASS OF THE LORD'S SUPPER

Just as the Paschal Triduum sets the tone for the entire liturgical year in a parish, the Mass of the Lord's Supper sets the tone for the Paschal Triduum. There is no "official description" of what Holy Thursday is about in the church's liturgical documents; we have to derive its "meaning" from the source texts of the Missal and Lectionary.

The Mass of the Lord's Supper *is*:

- *The opening of the Triduum*, and not simply a liturgy unto itself. Rather than narrowly focused on any one particular "theme," the Mass of the Lord's Supper is our entrance into the great three days. In the *entrance antiphon*, the official opening musical text for this Mass, we might expect to see something eucharistic in focus, or related to the ministerial priesthood, or recalling the Last Supper. Rather, we sing an introduction to the whole three days: "We should glory in the Cross of our Lord Jesus Christ, / in whom is our salvation, life and resurrection, / through whom we are saved and delivered" (Roman Missal, Thursday of the Lord's Supper 6). The Mass of the Lord's Supper is the first stage of a multiday sacred festival focused on the death and Resurrection of Christ.

- *The parish Mass of the day.* There is no morning Mass in the parish—there are no texts in the Missal for such a Mass because one is not envisioned. Your diocese may still celebrate the chrism Mass with the bishop on this morning, but in most places this diocesan celebration is held on a more convenient day earlier in Lent. All who wish to celebrate Holy Thursday—clergy and laity—participate in this one Mass in the evening. In fact, it is one of the specific instances in which concelebration by priests is encouraged, and no Masses without the faithful are even permitted. All ministers should be invited to participate, each fulfilling his or her own ministry in concert with others.

- *Not a reenactment of the night before Jesus died.* Liturgy is not about re-creating historical events. Our holy remembering takes place conscious of these events of history being made present again in our midst. On this night, when we keep watch, when we wash feet, when we break bread and share a common cup, we do not simply "playact" the biblical narrative.

- *Related to, but distinct from, Good Friday.* It would be a mistake to see Holy Thursday's evening Mass of the Lord's Supper as merely a prelude to the liturgy of Good Friday, as if one were more important than the other. On its own, the Passion is not the sum total of the paschal mystery—the Resurrection is essential to this mystery. Holy Thursday's Mass recalls the institution of the Eucharist, of the ministerial priesthood, and the Gospel command of service; these are related to, but distinct from, the motifs of Good Friday.

- *Multivalent.* In this liturgy, the themes of sacrifice, Eucharist, charity, redemption, service, and sacred banquet are all intertwined and hang together coherently.

In some ways, this Mass is like a festive Sunday Eucharist, but there are many important details to consider. You'll find a checklist of important preparation details in the appendix, but there are a few significant things that make this Mass different from a typical Sunday Eucharist.

Timing

What time should this liturgy begin? The Roman Missal simply notes that it takes place at a "convenient" time in the evening. It could take place at the same time as a typical holy day of obligation evening Mass, so as not to confuse people. It could begin at a different time, to set it apart. To begin at the time of a typical Saturday evening Mass anticipating Sunday would likely be too early on a weekday to allow for most people to participate. To wait until the start time of the Easter Vigil, which follows in two days, would be very late.

Consider what's happening before Mass. Are people hurrying home from work and school (in many cases, the last day before a holiday break), and making dinner quickly before coming to church? Maybe there's a parish supper that makes it easier for the faithful to eat before Mass, and sets a tone of festivity for the evening. How much time will ministers need to prepare?

Art and Environment

Consider how the environment for worship sets the tone for this important evening liturgy. The church should look and feel different from both Lent and Easter: one has concluded, one is yet to begin. The altar (and church) can be decorated with flowers, but in moderation—Easter has not yet come. Simple, clean, beautiful linens, vestments, and candles help mark the importance of this time as a "hinge" between Lent and Easter.

The baptismal font and holy water stoups are emptied; they will be refilled in preparation for the Easter Vigil. (If you've had them empty since Lent began, make a note that next year water can remain during Lent, a season focused on baptism.)

The pitchers, bowls, and towels for the footwashing could be displayed prominently in the liturgical decor, in anticipation of this ritual, which is described below. (Pro tip: if you fill a pitcher with scalding hot water shortly before Mass begins, it will be comfortably warm after the homily.)

The tabernacle is empty: Communion on Good Friday will come from the bread consecrated tonight. Prior to Mass beginning, consume any of the Blessed Sacrament that remains in the tabernacle or, if necessary, use it for the Communion of some of the faithful on the previous Monday, Tuesday, or Wednesday.

If the Blessed Sacrament will be solemnly adored tonight in its usual place of reposition, make sure it's festively decorated and prepared for the procession. If adoration will take place in another location (the merits of which are discussed below), make sure that place is beautiful and worthy.

If the oils from the chrism Mass are to be borne in procession (see below), they can be placed either in the ambry, their usual spot, or another special place of honor during Mass; consider placing them near the altar, to show the intimate connection between all the sacraments.

Introductory Rites and Liturgy of the Word

Before Mass begins, there will likely be a different "feel" in the church from a typical Sunday or weekday Mass. A buzz of excitement will likely be palpable. Many ministers will be earnestly preparing for their duties during this liturgy. Parishioners who regularly attend different Sunday Mass times—and consequently haven't seen each other for a while—will want to catch up.

All of this is good and needed. However, make sure that the worship space has a suitable calm and a mood conducive to prayer. Hospitality ministers can help establish this tone at the doors to the nave, and if ministers have rehearsed earlier in the week, last-minute worries should be minimal.

MUSIC TIP: Prelude music will help to establish a solemn and special feel for tonight; remember that tonight isn't about any "one thing"—if you have sung texts, they should reflect the diversity of themes celebrated tonight and during these three days (see beginning of this chapter).

Even if you don't typically have a "call to worship" read before Mass, consider one this night. A pastoral minister, a community leader (parish council member), or even the pastor himself might welcome everyone— especially visitors and guests—and explain *very briefly* the meaning of the Triduum and how tonight's liturgy opens it. If there are important liturgical details, which need to be explained verbally, this is a much better time than during the liturgy itself. If the pastor does this from the front of church, he could simply invite people to some quiet contemplation in sacred silence while he returns to the back of church, vests in a chasuble, and prepares for the entrance procession.

MUSIC TIP: The entrance antiphon for this night establishes well the main motif for not just the Mass of the Lord's Supper but for the entire Triduum. Consider a musical setting that will allow this text, or something similar, to be sung by the entire assembly to open this evening's liturgy.

Incense should be used on this night. It leads a procession of cross, candles, deacon, concelebrating priests, and presiding priest. If you typically include other lay ministers (e.g., lectors, extraordinary ministers of Holy Communion) in the entrance procession, they could be included tonight as usual. Other ministers exercising a function tonight (e.g., those assisting with the footwashing ritual) could be included in the procession as well.

If the newly blessed and consecrated oils of catechumens and the infirm, and the sacred chrism are to be received solemnly by the parish, this Mass is a possible time (since the chrism Mass likely just happened recently). Previous editions of the Roman Missal expected that the oils would be received, and offered a specific text for this ritual. The current edition does not specify how or when this would happen, but they could simply be carried in tonight's entrance procession to a prepared place (as described above.) The oil-bearer carries the oil aloft, pausing in front of the altar to show the oil to the people, and takes it to the prepared place. A person recently anointed and restored to health might carry the oil of the sick; one of the adults to be baptized on Saturday could carry the oil of catechumens. A candidate for confirmation or holy orders could bear the sacred chrism.

 ART & ENVIRONMENT TIP: For festivity, decorate the place of reposition for the oils with the colors traditionally associated with them (green for sick, purple for catechumens, gold for chrism).

The greeting and the act of penitence take place in the usual way. The Gloria in Excelsis is sung tonight. By tradition, church bells are rung during the Gloria and are then silent until the same hymn is sung during the Easter Vigil.

 MUSIC TIP: If your parish has a handbell choir, they could ring on the Gloria both nights to honor this tradition.

The collect is then chanted or recited in the usual way. If the presiding priest sings reasonably well, consider chanted greetings, dialogues, and orations for tonight's solemn liturgy.

The Liturgy of the Word takes place in the usual way with readings from Exodus and First Corinthians, Psalm 116, and the Gospel of John. The Book of the Gospels can be used tonight.

 DEACON TIP: If a deacon or concelebrating priest sings well, consider chanting the gospel on this solemn night.

 PREACHING TIP: Notably, the Missal specifies that the priest gives a homily (not optional) "in which light is shed on the principal mysteries that are commemorated in this Mass," including the institution of the Eucharist, the ministerial priesthood, and charity (Roman Missal, Thursday of the Lord's Supper 9).

Mandatum

In many Christian communities, Holy Thursday is known by the traditional name "Maundy Thursday," related to the gospel of the day: Jesus' *command* that we must wash the feet of others. Those who lead must serve. The great must become humble. At the Last Supper, Jesus gives us the example.

The ancient ritual of washing of feet is called the *Mandatum* and traditionally takes place on Holy Thursday. Throughout history, this ritual has not always taken place, and not always during Mass itself. It is found in the current edition of the Missal, as an optional rite "where a pastoral reason suggests it." I would suggest that this powerful ancient symbol of service and humility is so intimately connected to the biblical institution of the Eucharist that one would need a compelling pastoral reason to omit it.

In his book *Washing Feet: Imitating the Example of Jesus in the Liturgy Today* (Liturgical Press, 2015), Thomas O'Loughlin carefully traces the Christian practice of footwashing throughout the centuries, exploring the significance of this gritty human ritual in our liturgical practice. Among the arguments O'Loughlin offers in support of liturgical footwashing is its gospel roots. It is very clear that Jesus commanded his disciples to "do this." O'Loughlin also points out that while the Eucharist has been and continues to be a sad source of division within the Christian community, footwashing remains common ground for all disciples of Jesus.

On this day, the Creed is not recited; the *Mandatum* takes place immediately following the sacred silence after the homily. The Missal describes how the presiding priest washes the feet of some selected men (*viri selecti*) with the assistance of some ministers. It does not specify how many sets of feet are washed: to avoid the appearance of "playacting" you might consider a number other than twelve.

In 2016, Pope Francis changed the rubrics for this ritual, not only allowing for both men *and* women to have their feet washed, but encouraging that those participating would reflect the diversity of the entire people of God. Prior to this new legislation changing the rubrics in the Roman Missal, many communities had already expanded this ritual of footwashing to include more than just twelve men; there are many options you could consider. Perhaps different people whose feet are to be washed would symbolically represent different groups within the community. Perhaps those ministers assisting with this ritual are pastoral ministers or members of leadership groups within the parish. One parish has their pastoral council members' feet washed by the pastor, and then, following his example, they wash the feet of anyone in the parish community who desires to come forward. Another parish has families come forward together to stations around the church and wash each other's feet; parents wash the feet of their children, and children wash the feet of their parents.

Depending on how many people will participate in this ritual, you may need multiple pitchers of water, bowls, and towels, as well as chairs or places for seating those whose feet will be washed. If you anticipate many people participating, you will need to refill the pitchers of water throughout the ritual, removing used towels, and draining basins that are full. Consider recruiting a stable group from within the parish—high school youth ministry members, altar servers, or a Bible study group—to facilitate this ritual gracefully and efficiently. This ritual should not feel hurried, but certainly shouldn't be so prolonged as to overshadow the other important ritual elements of the liturgy. Set up the stations (before Mass may work best) and direct the flow of traffic to avoid it seeming like everyone *must* participate: invitation is the key here. Make sure to clean up whatever is reasonably removed from aisles and floor space in anticipation of the Communion procession.

Singing should accompany the entire rite; it could alternate between the choir and the assembly. The Missal provides some antiphons based on the gospel of the day, which are recommended; many other lovely compositions exist as well.

As O'Loughlin points out, "For most Christians, footwashing is a form whose value and significance is awaiting discovery" (*Washing Feet*, 88). Perhaps your community needs to celebrate this ritual more frequently than just once a year, or to make time and opportunity for mystagogical reflection upon this deeply biblical ritual. As O'Loughlin so wonderfully summarizes, "The challenge of footwashing is that we all experience serving and being served, loving and being loved, and recognizing the new relationships that belong to the kingdom" (ibid., 60).

Following the washing of feet, the universal prayer takes place in the usual way.

Liturgy of the Eucharist

In all, the Liturgy of the Eucharist takes place like any other Mass. Make sure enough bread is prepared and brought to the altar tonight for the Communion of the faithful both tonight and during the Good Friday liturgy. If you don't typically have Communion under both kinds for all the faithful, consider doing so tonight.

The Roman Missal gives two hints about the preparation rite tonight: gifts for the poor could be included in the procession with bread and wine, and the antiphon *Ubi Caritas* (Where charity and love are found, God is there) is the preferred text to be sung. Invite parishioners to bring gifts of food, clothing, and money for the poor, and include it in the procession to the altar, a symbolic representation of the community's solidarity with the poor in this, and every, eucharistic celebration. One parish, rather than simply having a "representative" basket of food brought forward, invites everyone to come forward, placing canned goods and boxes of pasta around the altar—what an impressive display of the power of food, both earthly and heavenly!

If incense is being used tonight, lavish the altar, gifts, and cross with fragrant smoke. The presiding priest, concelebrants, and the assembly should also be honored with incense on this night when we celebrate the institution of the eucharistic sacrifice.

The first preface for the Most Holy Eucharist is with the other presidential texts for Holy Thursday, and focuses on the sacramental sacrifice of the Eucharist. A version of Eucharistic Prayer I is also here, with some language specific to this Mass. Even if you don't typically use this ancient and venerable text, or are tempted by one of the shorter eucharistic prayers due to the length of Mass, consider using the prayer envisioned by the Missal. Very few people are watching the clock tonight.

 PRESIDING TIP: This is a night to sing part or all of the eucharistic prayer. If it doesn't seem appropriate to sing the entire prayer, consider singing the preface with its dialogue, as well as the epiclesis and institution narrative, in addition to the usual sung acclamations by the people.

Even if you don't typically incense the consecrated host and chalice during the eucharistic prayer (done while the priest shows them to the people during the institution narrative), consider having the thurifer do this tonight, kneeling on the floor in front of the altar.

The Communion rite takes place as usual, albeit with more bread consecrated than is needed tonight. You might consider placing enough consecrated hosts for Good Friday's liturgy in a ciborium during the fraction rite, and setting it aside on the altar, rather than having all the consecrated bread divided among the Communion ministers. It would be better to break a few hosts for a big crowd tonight than not to have any left over for Good Friday, a day that typically sees bigger crowds than Holy Thursday.

After all have received Communion, any leftover consecrated bread is gathered into suitable vessels and remains on the altar. The consecrated bread set aside for Good Friday should be here as well. All other vessels should be taken to the credence table, sacristy, or some other suitable place for purification now or after Mass. The Missal is removed, and the Blessed Sacrament is all that remains on the altar—still covered with cloth and corporal—accompanied by lit candles.

The Transfer of the Most Blessed Sacrament

One of the most distinct features of the Holy Thursday Mass of the Lord's Supper is its conclusion. Rather than following the pattern of the usual concluding rites, Mass this night ends with a procession with the Blessed Sacrament to the place of reposition, and a period of solemn adoration. Functionally, since there is no Mass on Good Friday, the Blessed Sacrament has to be reserved the night before for Communion. Ritually, we solemnly bear the eucharistic bread to a place of reposition so we can keep vigil in adoration throughout the night.

Prior to the 1955 Holy Week reforms, it was understood in some places that the reposition of the Blessed Sacrament in the tabernacle at this time on this night was in imitation of placing the Lord's body in the tomb. The closing of the door was like the guards sealing the tomb. The adoration that followed was like that of the faithful women. The entire sequence of reposing the Blessed Sacrament on Holy Thursday night was funereal.

As Patrick Regan rightfully notes in his book *Advent to Pentecost* (Liturgical Press, 2012), the character of this ritual is not funereal (165). Regan points out that even the circular letter from Rome on the Triduum, *Paschalis Sollemnitatis*, states clearly, "The place where the tabernacle or pyx is situated must not be made to resemble a tomb, and the expression *tomb* is to be avoided for the chapel of repose is not prepared so as to represent the 'Lord's burial' but for the custody of the eucharistic bread that will be distributed in communion on Good Friday" (*PS* 55).

ART & ENVIRONMENT TIP: It will be important for ministers to decorate this place of repose not as for a funeral.

Look for opportunities to catechize the faithful about the nature of the conclusion of the Holy Thursday liturgy, helping them see it not as mimicking the entombment of Jesus, but rather the worship of Christ present in sacrament and the connection with the Holy Communion of both Thursday and Friday.

The Roman Missal prescribes the order of this procession, who's involved, and exactly what takes place. You should consult these rubrics and enflesh this ritual in your church as best you can. This is not *exposition*: a ciborium, rather than a monstrance, is used. The altar of repose is decorated simply and modestly.

Consider a procession to a place outside the main church for the reposition of the Blessed Sacrament. Perhaps you have a reservation chapel or smaller chapel. Perhaps you have a large community room that could be set up with the altar of repose. Perhaps all the faithful present at Mass could join in the procession to this other place, led by torchbearers in the darkness, singing a simple Taizé chant like "Stay here and keep watch with me." Hospitality ministers will be needed to help the crowd of people move gracefully and safely.

A "chapel of repose" large enough for the entire liturgical assembly would allow for everyone to process, and then spend some time in solemn adoration. Once the procession has entered the space, the presider—who has borne the Blessed Sacrament, preceded by incense—places the ciborium in the tabernacle on the altar of repose, and then incenses it while kneeling. The assembly will likely kneel as the presiding priest does. All could sing the traditional chant *Tantum Ergo* now.

 PRESIDING TIP: Make sure the presider and other ministers spend at least a few minutes in solemn silent adoration, modeling for everyone else this important ritual of the night.

After the ministers leave, the faithful can remain in solemn adoration until midnight. Take note that there is no concluding blessing or dismissal tonight: the liturgy "continues" with Good Friday's celebration of the Lord's Passion, rather than truly "ending" tonight. The candles that accompanied the procession should remain here and lit. Passages from the Gospel of John's Last Supper discourse might be read occasionally, every thirty minutes or so. The period of solemn adoration could conclude with a communal celebration of Night Prayer (Compline).

Even though solemn adoration ends at Midnight (blow out candles except perhaps one to indicate the Blessed Sacrament's presence, remove some flowers, etc.), adoration could continue throughout the night, and in fact right up until the celebration of the Lord's Passion on Good Friday. If Morning Prayer (Lauds) is prayed on Good Friday, it could take place in this chapel of repose. If your parish has a perpetual adoration ministry throughout the year, invite them to rally people to adore the Blessed Sacrament throughout the night until the Good Friday liturgy begins.

Before You Head Home . . .

The altar in the church is stripped after Mass, not as part of the Mass. All linens, flowers, and other decor are removed in anticipation of the Good Friday liturgy, which takes place with a bare altar and church stripped of flowers. If the oils were displayed elsewhere during tonight, take them to the ambry. The church should look stark and empty, and should now be ready for the celebration of the Lord's Passion, the traditional Good Friday liturgy.

4

Good Friday
Celebration of
the Lord's Passion

Having entered into the Paschal Triduum through the Mass of the Lord's Supper, we now turn our attention to Good Friday, with its celebration of the Lord's Passion. This principal liturgy is usually better attended than the Holy Thursday Mass or the Easter Vigil. In the United States and other Judeo-Christian cultures, Good Friday has traditionally been a day off work and school for many people, enabling their participation at church.

Throughout history, Good Friday has been a day like no other in the church's calendar: it is the only day of the year on which Mass may not be celebrated at all. The Roman Missal directs that the sacraments are not celebrated, except for penance and anointing of the sick. There may be no "Communion service," and Holy Communion is given only within the celebration of the Lord's Passion, or brought to the sick who cannot attend that liturgy.

Timing

Throughout history, the Good Friday liturgy has taken place at various times during the day. The current rubrics of the Roman Missal direct that it takes place about three o'clock, unless a later hour is chosen for a pastoral reason. This start time is, of course, associated closely with the biblical account of Jesus' death. You might consider a later start time if it enables a great number of people to participate who would otherwise be at work or in school. The rubrics even permit the principal liturgy to be repeated, with the permission of the bishop. If your parish already sees a full church at the afternoon liturgy, you might consider asking to repeat the celebration of the Lord's Passion in the evening, to enable more participation by the faithful on this holy day.

Let me offer a word about the pace of this liturgy. Freed from the schedule of parish Sunday mornings, and attended—without obligation—only by those who truly want to be there, make sure this liturgy never feels rushed. Generous periods of sacred silence are envisioned before, during, and after: do this well. It will be important for everyone to be able to contemplate the true significance of this liturgy and its powerful rituals.

Art and Environment

When we left church last night, the altar was stripped of linens and flowers. The Missal specifies that before the Good Friday liturgy begins, the altar has no candles, cross, or cloth. The sanctuary should look stark and bare, a contrast to both Holy Thursday and Eastertide. Any crosses could be removed from the church or veiled in fabric.

Ministers

While this liturgy is not Mass, a priest must still lead it. There have been questions raised about why a parish deacon could not preside for this celebration, but those have been clearly answered by a new rubric in the third edition of the Roman Missal. This makes sense because Good Friday is the second part of a multi-movement series of liturgies, beginning on Holy Thursday and concluding with Easter. The structure of the liturgy itself (as we will see below) shows how this service begins *in medias res* and ends without conclusion.

A parish priest presides for this liturgy, assisted by a deacon if present. There is no concelebration since this is not a eucharistic liturgy, so other priests should vest in an alb and stole or choir dress, and be seated in a suitable place among the faithful.

You should plan for the numbers and kinds of lay ministers you normally have for a Sunday liturgy in your parish, with a few exceptions. First, Communion today is given only under the form of bread, so you won't need any extraordinary ministers for the chalice. Second, you might benefit from an additional server or two, depending on how many you typically have ministering (see below for details). Finally, since this is not Mass, you won't need any gift-bearers. Other ministers—lectors, greeters, musicians, and so forth—are needed to fulfill their ministries like a Sunday or holy day liturgy.

As we discussed in chapter 2, a master of ceremonies might be valuable today, especially since the Good Friday liturgy is unique and celebrated only once a year. Without the typical contours of Mass for everyone to follow, an MC might be very helpful in guiding all the ordained and lay ministers through a reverent celebration of the Lord's Passion.

Introductory Rites and Liturgy of the Word

Just like the night before, prior to the Good Friday liturgy there will likely be a different "feel" in the church from a typical Sunday or weekday Mass. Last night's buzz of excitement and flurry of activity will likely give way to a somber and reflective mood in the church. Make sure your church is open all day on Good Friday, because people will want to come in and pray (more details on this later).

All rehearsals for the liturgy, including warm-up by musicians, should conclude well before the liturgy is scheduled to begin. A half hour of silence in the church before the celebration is not too much to facilitate and encourage prayer and reflection on this somber day. Any preparation in the church or adjacent areas should be completed in the morning.

A printed worship aid is very helpful on this day because the order of service does not follow a typical pattern of Sunday Eucharist. If your parish designs and prints its own worship aid, make sure to include some liturgical catechesis about the day and what the church celebrates.

For example, you might explain why the Good Friday liturgy begins with no real entrance procession, and with no singing. Both of these will surely grab the attention of the liturgical assembly, so a word or two of explanation might be helpful. The Missal specifies that the priest and deacon, wearing red Mass vestments (chasuble and dalmatic), go to the altar in silence and, after making a reverence like usual, prostrate themselves before the altar. They could follow the route of the typical entrance procession for Mass, or—to further show the contrast between this day and every other day—the ministers could come to the altar from someplace else entirely.

Prostration is a profound gesture used only in the liturgy to represent profound humility, such as during the Litany of the Saints at an ordination. This prostration should be made by the priest and deacon lying flat, facedown, on the floor in front of the altar. The Missal does allow, if appropriate, for the priest and deacon to kneel rather than lay prostrate. However, the preferred sign better manifests our stance before God as we celebrate the Lord's Passion: true humility, just as Christ lowered himself before he was made great.

The duration of the prostration should be significant ("for a while"). Everyone else (including other ministers) kneels. This period of silent prayer should allow for everyone to adopt a comfortable posture, and then actually enter into a time of contemplation. Sixty seconds is not too long.

As the priest and deacon rise, they go to the chair. The faithful stand, and the opening prayer is spoken like the collect at Mass with one notable distinction: the invitation "Let us pray" does not precede it. This typical invitation is omitted because silence has preceded the oration—no more silence is needed for people to meditate. The absence of this invitation is, like the prostration and silence, a further distinction between today's solemn commemoration and "Mass as usual."

Notice that there is no sign of the cross, Pauline greeting, or any of the other typical opening rites, except the opening prayer. Because the celebration of the Lord's Passion begins where the Holy Thursday liturgy left off, it has no true "beginning" and, as we'll see later in this chapter, no true "ending."

After the opening prayer, all are seated for the Liturgy of the Word. If you typically dismiss young children to another space for a children's Liturgy of the Word on Sundays, omit it today. Not only is it important for everyone to celebrate the Liturgy of the Word together on this day, but it would be difficult to replicate the stark and somber mood of the main assembly in a gathering just for young children.

RCIA TIP: While we're speaking of dismissals, there is no reason that the elect—those catechumens preparing for baptism tomorrow—can't participate in this entire liturgy, without receiving Holy Communion. The eucharistic prayer—a right and duty of the baptized—is obviously not part of the Good Friday liturgy.

The first reading, responsorial psalm, and second reading take place in the usual way. These readings do not change from year to year, and have a traditional association with this day. Make sure the lectors are well prepared to proclaim these lengthy and weighty passages. The psalmist must be prepared to sing Psalm 31, giving voice to Christ's pleading with the Father.

An acclamation other than Alleluia can be sung before the gospel, just like during Lent.

MUSIC TIP: To continue to make it clear that the Triduum is not part of Lent, consider choosing a different acclamation for Holy Thursday and Good Friday than was sung during the forty days prior. If you can't muster a different acclamation, perhaps singing it unaccompanied or making some other adjustment to the musical performance would help reinforce the seasonal distinction.

The Passion according to John is proclaimed today. The rubrics direct that this take place "as on the preceding [Palm] Sunday," so one must turn back a few chapters in the Missal to find the details on today's proclamation. First, there are no candles or incense used, no greeting "The Lord be with you . . . " or signing of the book. Multiple readers can be used, including the deacon and priest. A version in the *Lectionary for Mass* divides the narrative among four speakers, a narrator, other voices, the crowd, and Jesus. The priest should take the part of Christ. A deacon appropriately takes the role of the narrator. Other readers could take the voices of the other characters and the crowd, or these could be combined into one person reading alongside the priest and deacon.

While it is possible for the assembly to take the part of the crowd, this presents both logistical and theological issues. Unless your worship aid or missalette has the entire text of the Passion reproduced, the assembly will not know its parts. Furthermore, asking the assembly to "take a role" for which they have not prepared will find them focusing more on whether they're ready to "say their line" than focusing on the content of the Passion itself. The proclamation of Scripture in the liturgy is not Bible study or "readers' theater"; it is celebration of the embodied Word, present in our midst. Jesus Christ himself speaks to us when the Scriptures are read in the church, proclaimed with faith, and listened to in earnest. Let the people listen attentively to this central narrative of the Gospel, proclaimed by a few well-prepared ministers.

As I mentioned in chapter 2, the Passion could appropriately be sung. Musical settings have been composed in nearly every era for the sung proclamation of this important narrative. With some practice in the weeks beforehand, a few ministers who sing confidently could bring the Passion gospel truly alive with the heightened emphasis that singing brings to a text.

You can divide the Passion in any way you like, including by "scene," alternating readers each time the setting changes within the narrative. Consider what divisions will best help the faithful hear this iconic narrative and reflect upon it in their hearts.

Regardless of what format you choose, the Missal assumes that the faithful stand during the Passion, just as they do for any liturgical proclamation of the gospel. Those who need to sit for the whole, or even part, of the proclamation will do so, but the assembly should remain standing insofar as it is possible.

After the Passion has concluded, all are seated (some with an audible sigh of relief!) and the priest gives "a brief homily." Even though this is not Mass, there is no permission for anyone but the presiding priest to preach.

PREACHING TIP: All good preachers know that a "brief" homily is much harder to prepare than a "regular" one. The homilist must work hard to prepare some words that will help connect the paschal mystery, the dying and rising of Christ, to the lives of the faithful in a special way on this annual commemoration of the Lord's Passion. Don't underestimate the power of these brief remarks.

The Missal also suggests that the faithful may be invited to spend a short time in prayer after the homily. If your parish doesn't normally observe a suitable period of silence after the homily, you should do so today, perhaps even explicitly noting this verbally or in the worship aid. A few minutes is not too long.

The Solemn Intercessions

An original feature of early eucharistic liturgies, the universal prayer (aka prayer of the faithful, or bidding prayers, or intercessions) disappeared from the Mass early in Western liturgical history. Restored to the Order of Mass for Sundays and weekdays with the liturgical reforms following the Second Vatican Council, they remained as part of the Good Friday liturgy all along.

Typically for Sundays and other Masses, there is great latitude in the number, topics, language, and format of the intercessions of the universal prayer. The *General Instruction of the Roman Missal* gives some simple parameters and trusts the local community to enflesh these prayers appropriately. In contrast, the solemn intercessions of the Good Friday liturgy are clearly defined in text, number, and format.

Truly "universal" in character, this ritual has changed throughout the centuries. Currently, there are prayers for the church and the pope, catechumens, the unity of Christians, the Jewish people, those in public office, those who don't believe in Christ or in God, and those "in tribulation."

There are ten prayers; the diocesan bishop "may permit or order the addition of a special intention" (Roman Missal, Friday of the Passion of the Lord 13). Note that there is no permission for a priest or local parish community to alter the number, content, or order of these intentions. And for good reason: these universal intentions unite the whole church on this important day, and are part of our liturgical tradition.

Each prayer has an "intention" that is announced—sung or spoken—by the deacon or, in his absence, a lay minister (cantor or reader). The priest then prays a "collect-style" prayer to which everyone sings or says "Amen." Both chant notation and text without music are found in the Roman Missal.

DEACON TIP: The Missal specifies that the deacon announces the intentions at the ambo, but this will require an additional copy of the text for him. If your deacon normally announces the intentions of the universal prayer standing to the right of the priest at the chair, this is possible today as well.

These intentions are lengthy and will require some preparation by both priest and deacon. It is possible to speak the intention and chant the collect-style prayer, if the deacon or other minister does not sing well but the priest does. This would have more solemnity than simply reciting the entire sequence of prayers.

The faithful all kneel or stand during the entire sequence of prayers, but it would be better to observe the traditional sequence of postures for these prayers. After he announces the intention, the deacon invites the people by singing or saying "Let us kneel." Then, after a suitable period of silence—in which the faithful meditate upon the intention and make it their own—the deacon sings or says "Let us stand," and the priest sings or says the collect-style prayer. This happens ten times. The posture changes may feel awkward at first, but by number ten, the community will have adopted a comfortable rhythm and can truly enter into prayer.

The response of the faithful to each of these ten solemn intercessions is simply a sung or spoken "Amen"; the rubrics do not envision any other litanic response.

The Adoration of the Holy Cross

One of the most distinctive and memorable features of the Good Friday celebration of the Lord's Passion is the adoration (or veneration) of the cross. Based on the ancient Roman liturgy in which the relics of the true cross were venerated by the pope and those gathered with him, the faithful who still gather annually on Good Friday venerate a cross, the principal Christian symbol, the instrument of our salvation. To this day the only times we genuflect to anything other than the Blessed Sacrament are at the words of the incarnation on the nativity and annunciation, and before the cross on Good Friday. We genuflect in adoration of the cross on Good Friday because we glory in the cross and the One who died upon it. As we sang at the beginning of last night's Mass of the Lord's Supper, it is through the cross that we are saved and set free.

The Missal provides two forms of the showing of the cross to the faithful before veneration, and generously suggests that the more appropriate one be chosen according to pastoral needs.

The first form sees the deacon or another suitable minister carrying a cross veiled in violet through the church to the middle of the sanctuary, accompanied by ministers with lighted candles. The priest meets them and ritually uncovers the cross, chanting the acclamation "Behold the wood of the Cross . . . " three times. Each time, the people respond, "Come, let us adore," and kneel for a short time in silent adoration of the cross (Friday of the Passion of the Lord 15).

The second form is like the first, but allows for the priest or deacon or another minister to carry an uncovered cross in procession like above. In this second form, the procession stops three times: near the doors of the church, in the middle of the church, and at the "entrance to the sanctuary." At each of the three stops, the acclamation and response are sung. As in the other form, all kneel in silent adoration as the one carrying the cross elevates it.

Either form is possible. If the crosses in your church have been veiled during Lent (or even just during the final days), consider the first form. To make a clear connection between today's liturgy and the Easter Vigil, to connect cross and paschal candle, consider the second form because the locations for stopping and singing the acclamation can be exactly the same on both days.

Regardless of the form used for showing the cross, adoration of the holy cross now takes place. The Missal explains clearly who does what and how. Notice that only one cross may be used for veneration. If the number of people is so great that individuals coming forward to venerate the cross is not possible, the priest can simply invite the assembly together, in their places, to adore the cross for a while in silence. This second option is less than desirable, but speaks well to the liturgical preference for one noble and beautiful symbol, rather than a multiplication of them. Only one cross— large, noble, sturdy, and worthy—is for the veneration of the community.

The Missal suggests that after the priest and other ministers venerate the cross, everyone else comes forward in a kind of procession to do the same. If a large cross is used, there is no reason that it can't be approached from all sides. Make sure the candles that accompanied the cross and remain are far enough away to permit access from multiple sides. In many cases, family units come together to the cross, mom and dad modeling a kiss or other reverent gesture of veneration for their children.

 PRESIDING TIP: The Missal also suggests that the priest could remove his shoes, a symbol of humility, before adoring the cross. There is no reason that the faithful couldn't do the same.

This ritual is utterly simple, and does not need to be elaborated in any way. The most simple cross and the most simple acts of veneration will speak more loudly than any contrived "enhancements" we might attempt.

Note that the object for veneration is described as being a "cross" and not a "crucifix." Since this ritual descends from the adoration of relics of the true cross, a cross made of wood—perhaps by members of your local community—may be the best choice. Choose a wood light enough to be carried without too much trouble, but hard enough to last for generations.

 ART & ENVIRONMENT TIP: This cross could be displayed during Lent, or at least its last few weeks, and then lovingly adored on Good Friday. The cross could also be displayed during Eastertide, adorned with lilies and other Easter flowers. This cross can be put away during the balance of the year, but treated with care.

After the adoration of the cross during this liturgy is concluded, it is taken by the deacon or another minister to a place of honor near the altar, and remains accompanied by lit candles.

During the time of adoration of the cross, there should be singing.

 MUSIC TIP: Remember, Good Friday is not a funeral liturgy; the very title "Celebration" of the Lord's Passion should help us remember that we commemorate the Lord's death, but—as always—we celebrate his Resurrection too! Singing can help bring a sense of joy, even if restrained, to this element of the liturgy.

The Missal provides some traditional texts to be sung during the adoration of the cross. There are several musical settings, in various styles, of these texts published and available for your community to learn and sing. The rubrics permit "other suitable chants" to be used, but consider using the traditional texts—the antiphon "We adore your cross, O Lord," the Reproaches, and the hymn "Faithful Cross"—before you seek alternatives. Any other texts to be sung should do what these preferred texts do: celebrate the entire paschal mystery, rather than simply treat the Passion alone.

Singing can be led by cantors or choir, and can certainly include the assembly at least on simple refrains. If unaccompanied singing isn't possible this day, make sure the musical accompaniment is simple and sparse, intended only to support the singing. Make sure there is profound musical contrast between this day and Easter!

Holy Communion

In the earliest days, the Eucharist was not celebrated on Good Friday, and Communion was not received. Over time, a simple Communion rite was added to the traditional liturgy of the day to satisfy the spiritual hunger of the faithful, if not their material hunger as fasting traditionally took place during the days of the Triduum. In time, the Lord's Prayer and other preparatory prayers before Communion were added, and the liturgy of the day came to be known as the "Mass of the Presanctified" because Communion was received from the bread consecrated the night before.

We have evidence from the patristic age that the sacraments were simply not celebrated on Good Friday, which would include reception of the Eucharist. In the Roman Rite, even when the faithful had begun to receive Communion on Good Friday out of increasing devotion, the papal liturgy resisted. Eighth-century liturgical texts indicate clearly that the pope and deacons did not receive Communion. Over time, however, a Communion rite similar to that of Mass made its way into sacramentaries.

Emblematic of an era where the faithful rarely received Communion anyway, by 1622 it was codified that only the ministers received Communion on Good Friday, not the faithful. It wasn't until the Holy Week reforms of 1955 that the faithful would again receive Communion on Good Friday.

Today's Good Friday celebration of the Lord's Passion includes a Communion rite that looks much like a typical Mass, except for a few notable exceptions. First, Communion is under the form of bread alone; the Precious Blood is not reserved from the Mass of the Lord's Supper. Second, there is no exchange of a sign of peace, a ritual intimately connected with the celebration of the Eucharist, not simply with the reception of Holy Communion. Finally, since the consecrated bread has already been broken, there is no fraction rite and no singing of the litany "Lamb of God . . . "

The Roman Missal provides very clear text and rubrics for how the Communion rite proceeds. The deacon, or in his absence the priest, puts on a humeral veil and goes to the altar of repose from the night before. He then brings the Blessed Sacrament back to the altar by the most direct route, which is not necessarily the route used last night for the festive procession. Two ministers with lighted candles accompany the Blessed Sacrament, and the candles go on or near the altar.

DEACON TIP: If the altar of repose from last night is not near the main altar of the church, the deacon and ministers with candles might even "sneak out" during the last part of the adoration of the cross by the faithful, especially if they can do so unnoticed. That way, the "procession" of the Blessed Sacrament back into the church can begin quickly after adoration of the cross concludes, rather than being preceded by a procession of the ministers out of the church (and awkward silence while the people wonder what is happening!).

While the ministers are going to retrieve the Blessed Sacrament, other ministers (not the presiding priest, but other ministers) should clothe the altar with a cloth and corporal, placing the Missal on the altar. An additional server or two might be especially helpful now, so that the altar can be prepared reverently, yet efficiently, while other ministers accompany the Blessed Sacrament. The preparation of the altar is more *functional* today, not *symbolic*, so it may be helpful to rehearse the ministers so that it unfolds with choreographed grace.

 ART & ENVIRONMENT TIP: Choose an altar cloth that is simple and perhaps one that reveals more of the altar than is normally seen. Make sure the ministers who will unfold it on the altar practice this, folding the cloth and placing it on the credence table so it can be easily carried and unfolded with style and grace.

If multiple people will minister Communion, the consecrated bread will need to be apportioned onto several plates. Do this right after the Blessed Sacrament is brought to the altar, rather than interrupting the flow of the prayers before Communion. The deacon should do all of this, assisted by other ministers as needed. Once the deacon has prepared the altar and the consecrated bread for distribution to the faithful, the priest goes to the altar.

The Missal specifies that during Communion, Psalm 22 or another suitable song may be sung. This could be any of your usual Communion processional psalms or songs, especially those that speak most strongly of the paschal mystery. Or, if your community regularly sings with gusto during

Communion, the absence of singing and a reverent silence would be noticeable. It could help reinforce that today's liturgy is unlike any other: not a celebration of the Eucharist, but a reception of Communion as spiritual food to sustain our paschal fast. Paul Turner, in his book *Glory in the Cross* (Liturgical Press, 2011), points out that since the Second Vatican Council, the rubrics for this liturgy have never required singing during Communion on Good Friday, and that there is a long tradition behind receiving Communion in silence on this day. Some drafts of the postconciliar liturgy even prohibited singing at this point, but ultimately singing was permitted as an option (*Glory in the Cross*, 107).

After Communion is finished, ideally all the consecrated bread has been consumed. Practically speaking, this may not happen. You may want to reserve a few pieces of consecrated bread for Viaticum Friday night and during the day on Saturday. You can either reserve this elsewhere after Thursday's evening Mass, or make sure there is some left over after Communion on Good Friday.

Any of the Blessed Sacrament that remains after Communion on Good Friday is then borne from the altar "to a place prepared outside the church" by the deacon, without solemnity (no humeral veil or candles), in a simple way. If there is no suitable place for reservation outside the church, the Blessed Sacrament could be reserved in the tabernacle, but this is less than ideal. A locked cupboard in a sacristy, accompanied by a simple votive candle, will serve as a suitable place for reservation overnight Friday and during the day on Saturday, and will be conveniently accessible to a priest needing to minister Viaticum to anyone dying during the Triduum.

A period of silent prayer takes place, followed by a post-Communion prayer in the usual way (including the invitation "Let us pray," omitted earlier in the liturgy). There is then a simple prayer over the people. Note in the Missal the absence of a greeting: the deacon or, in his absence, the priest simply invites the people to "bow down for the blessing."

All then genuflect to the cross and depart in silence. There is no final trinitarian blessing, dismissal, or concluding hymn. Just as it started as a continuation of the night prior, it ends without conclusion; this community will gather again on Saturday night to pick up where they left off.

Remove the cloth and corporal from the altar, leaving it once again bare. The cross should remain on or near the altar, with two or four lit candles. The cross is now an object of veneration by the faithful, honored with a genuflection after the principal liturgy, throughout the evening, and even overnight and through the day on Holy Saturday. Make sure the church continues to be open for the balance of Good Friday and during the day on Holy Saturday if it's feasible to do so.

If your parish has a reservation chapel for the Blessed Sacrament, it could be used as a place of adoration of the cross after the celebration of the Lord's

Passion and even overnight and during the day on Holy Saturday. Obviously the Blessed Sacrament is not reserved there following the Good Friday liturgy until after the Easter Vigil, so the cross could be given central place and adorned with lit candles. Encourage the faithful to spend time in adoration of the cross during this time.

5

The Easter Vigil in the Holy Night

We began chapter 3 talking about what the Mass of the Lord's Supper is; before we delve into preparing the Easter Vigil, let's examine what it *is*:

- *The high point of the Triduum.* The Easter Vigil is the center and heart of the three-day Paschal Triduum. Our festive entry on Holy Thursday, our solemn commemoration on Good Friday, and our fasting during Holy Saturday all prepare us for what has traditionally been called "the mother of all vigils."

- *The first Mass of Easter Sunday.* The Easter Vigil in the Holy Night is not an anticipated Mass for Sunday, like a typical Saturday evening Mass. The Easter Vigil is the opening of the fifty-day Eastertide festival.

- *The summit of the paschal cycle.* The ninety-day arc from Ash Wednesday until Pentecost reaches its summit at the Easter Vigil. Our Lenten and Eastertide seasons hinge at the Easter Vigil, where preparation and celebration come together.

- *The center of the parish's initiation ministry.* The Easter Vigil has long been the privileged moment throughout the entire year for the baptism of new Christians. Adult baptism takes place on other days with only serious pastoral need, so strong is the connection between the annual paschal feast and the sacrament of baptism.

- *A liturgy for the whole parish.* The restoration of the baptismal catechumenate and the promulgation of the Rite of Christian Initiation of Adults (RCIA) are among the greatest fruits of the liturgical movement of the twentieth century. Reestablishing the inseparable bond between adult baptism and the Easter Vigil has served the church well for decades now. However, one unfortunate result has been that, in some cases, the Easter Vigil seems a liturgy mostly for those directly associated with initiation. It's the "RCIA Mass," or simply a special Mass for those being baptized and their families. Not helped in this regard by its length and start time, the Easter Vigil is rarely seen as an equally attractive option as a Mass on Easter Sunday morning, and it takes tremendous energy on the part of pastoral ministers to counter that misunderstanding. Yet the Easter Vigil is the most important liturgy of the year for the entire parish.

- *Long.* There's no way to spin the fact that when celebrated well, the Easter Vigil is long—likely the longest liturgy of the entire year. But the Easter Vigil celebrated well is worth it.

The Easter Vigil in the Holy Night is a complex liturgy, shaped by tradition, restored to primacy by the Holy Week reforms of the 1950s. It has four principal parts.

The *Lucernarium*, or Service of Light, begins this beautiful liturgy. The people gather outside around a blazing fire and light the new paschal candle, which they then follow into the darkened church. They listen to a hymn of praise to Christ, the Light of the World, while holding lit candles. The light of Christ dispels the darkness of death: this is the Easter proclamation of Good News.

The *Liturgy of the Word* is the fullest liturgical commemoration of salvation history. Beginning with the story of creation, God's love story with the human race unfolds in sacred narrative. The people respond by singing psalms of praise. Paul's letter to the Romans is proclaimed, in which Christ's triumph over death is inexplicably linked to the sacrament of baptism. After the Alleluia, which disappeared forty days ago, returns by solemn intonation, the Resurrection account is proclaimed from the gospel. Jesus' Resurrection from the dead is the centerpiece of the entire Bible; tonight's Liturgy of the Word celebrates that blessed reality!

The *Baptismal Liturgy*, or Liturgy of Initiation, welcomes new Christians through the celebration of baptism and confirmation. Preceded by the Litany of the Saints and blessing of fresh water, catechumens are plunged into the waters of new birth, clothed with a white garment, and anointed with sacred chrism. The faithful are invited to renew their own baptismal vows, and are sprinkled with baptismal water.

Finally, the *Liturgy of the Eucharist* celebrates in sacramental sacrifice the saving mystery of Christ's death and Resurrection, at the high point of the year. The newly baptized participate for the first time in the Eucharist, and First Holy Communion, the culmination of their initiation.

The Easter Vigil is, undoubtedly, the most complicated liturgy of the year to prepare. More than any other, advance preparation is essential, and the collaboration of many, many ministers is the key to success. As with the other principal liturgies of the Triduum, a detailed checklist of remote and immediate preparation tasks can be found in the appendices.

Let's look at some issues to consider early on in your preparation process.

Timing

The Easter Vigil must start after dark. Period. The Roman Missal directs that it take place after nightfall of Saturday and before daybreak of Sunday. The Easter Vigil is entirely different from the anticipated Mass for Sunday, and most likely can't even begin at the same time on Saturday afternoon as your weekly anticipated Mass would. Good. There cannot be a Mass on Holy Saturday earlier than the Easter Vigil. This is, of course, for good reasons that the liturgy itself makes abundantly clear.

The timing of the Easter Vigil, and indeed Easter itself, is so closely aligned with the rhythm of the cosmos. We must wait until after the vernal equinox, when the darkness of winter wanes and the light returns. We wait until the Sunday following the new moon. We wait until after dark to begin. The earth, the sun, and the moon must all be ready to celebrate Christ—in whom all things were created, move, live, and have their being—and his victory over the darkness of sin and death.

Art and Environment

Throughout the day on Holy Saturday, following the Good Friday celebration of the Lord's Passion, the church remains stark; the altar is bare, flowers removed. The challenge for the art and environment team will be to prepare for the Easter Vigil during the day on Saturday, without disturbing the sense of Holy Saturday's stillness, prayer, and fasting. The Easter Vigil is the first Mass of Easter, and the church should be decorated as such. This will require forethought and advance planning.

The altar should be decorated with only those elements that cannot be "brought in" ritually during the liturgy itself. This may mean only a simple white cloth (with the gospel book on top of it, as this is not carried in procession tonight). We'll look below at how other linens, candles, and decorative elements could be added as the liturgy progresses, leading to a festively adorned altar.

Prepare the best versions of everything you have: the finest altar cloth, the most beautiful gold altar antependia, new tall candlesticks, the richest gold vestments, your most precious eucharistic vessels, the sweetest wine, the most fragrant incense. This is the night to use the "fine china"!

The baptismal font should be refilled during the day on Holy Saturday, in anticipation of baptism tonight. Even if no one will be baptized in your parish tonight, the font is still filled with fresh, clean water, which will be sprinkled on the people in renewal of their own baptism, and the font will be used throughout the year. Wait until after the Vigil concludes to fill any other dependent holy water stoups or vessels.

The tabernacle is still conspicuously empty, with no vigil light. Communion may be received on Holy Saturday only as Viaticum; only a few fragments of consecrated bread need to be reserved in a suitable place outside the church proper. Any of the Blessed Sacrament remaining after Communion tonight can be reposed in the usual tabernacle, and the vigil light relit *after* Mass.

The oils newly blessed and consecrated at the recent chrism Mass (and perhaps solemnly received by the parish on Holy Thursday) should be near the baptistery and ready for the liturgy of baptism.

The *new* paschal candle should be prepared for its inauguration tonight. Your best clean follower, incense grains, perhaps a wind-guard for the procession if you anticipate a gusty night—all these should be prepared in the vesting sacristy, or from wherever the ministers will leave for the blessing of the fire.

A place for the paschal candle should be prepared, ideally near the ambo. Even if it will be located elsewhere during the fifty-day Eastertide, the paschal candle stand should be next to the ambo tonight, if at all possible.

Your church has been busy for the past few days: make sure to sweep, vacuum, clean restrooms, tidy up pews, and so forth. Leave nothing untouched as you prepare for tonight's great feast!

Texts

A worship aid booklet for tonight's liturgy will be very important. Many people will be unfamiliar with the structure of the liturgy, which is unusual and only happens once a year. While the use of familiar psalms, litanies, responses, ritual music, and hymns is important, there are still so many unique elements that a single worship aid booklet will be of great value to the assembly. Even if you didn't prepare one for the earlier liturgies, consider making one for tonight. Include simple catechetical instructions that might help people to enter into the liturgy more fully.

To assist the presiding priest and other ministers, I highly recommend creating your own "missal" for this liturgy. Both the Rite of Christian Initiation of Adults and the Roman Missal are needed tonight by the presiding minister. Each includes many options, a multitude of rubrics, and plenty of instances of "in these or similar words." Additionally, the presider will need prepared texts in multiple locations (outside fire, chair, baptistery, altar) and toting around multiple books may not be reasonable. Names of those to be initiated and their companions will need to be accessible to the presiding priest as well.

There are entirely too many variables during this complicated, lengthy, once-a-year liturgy (part of which takes place in the dark!) to underestimate the value of a unified, prepared text. Figure out which options will be used, which rubrics need to be seen during the liturgy itself, and craft any needed words of introduction or explanation rather than improvise. This will also allow you to insert musical notation as desired, since this night calls for as much singing by the priest as can reasonably be done. Create one integrated text and place it in a beautiful binder or folder. Make sure all involved have a copy of this "script" so everyone's literally "on the same page."

The *Lectionary for Mass* should be preset on the ambo, with the readings to be used marked clearly. Since the structure of the Liturgy of the Word tonight is different, anything you can do to assist the lectors in knowing their role will be helpful.

The Book of the Gospels is not carried in the entrance procession, and should be preset on the altar in its usual place. Mark it ahead of time for the proper gospel, and include chant notation if it will be sung (and, on this night, why wouldn't it be?!).

The *Exsultet* proclamation should be prepared at the chair of the deacon who will sing it, or at the ambo, or some other suitable place. There are fine-bound editions of this important liturgical text that you can purchase, or put a copy of the musical notation in a worthy binder yourself. Make sure the singer's notes are in there.

The Psalter should be at the ambo, ready for the psalmists who will lead singing during the Liturgy of the Word. Make sure everyone knows where to find everything they need before the liturgy begins.

Ministers

More ministers will be needed tonight than perhaps for any other liturgy your parish celebrates all year. Make sure you choose the best ones, and help them prepare well for their awesome tasks tonight.

The presiding priest should be one who not only has "read the black" and is prepared to "do the red" but has immersed himself in the deeper internal significance of the Easter Vigil, really that of the entire Paschal Triduum. He must lead the people tonight in the most important eucharistic liturgy of the year; a profound understanding of how the many rituals of the Easter Vigil are connected is important for an authentic and effective ministry as presider tonight.

Two deacons will both be very busy in their ministry tonight; it could be overwhelming for only one deacon. Consider one to be primary deacon for the light ritual and Liturgy of the Word (carrying the paschal candle, sing-ing the *Exsultet* and chanting the Gospel), and one to be the primary deacon for the liturgies of initiation and Eucharist (assisting with baptism while the other one carries the paschal candle to the baptistery, announcing the intentions of the universal prayer, performing the usual diaconal functions during the Liturgy of the Eucharist, and singing the Easter dismissal with double Alleluias).

Make sure the deacons are well prepared for their duties this night. Physi-cally "walking through" important ritual moments (like the procession with the candle or the procession to the baptistery) will be very important, and better done earlier in the week than thirty minutes before the Vigil begins.

Other priests in the parish should be invited to concelebrate. They can take parts of the eucharistic prayer and minister Holy Communion. If your assembly or building is large, one of them could assist the presiding priest in sprinkling the assembly with baptismal water.

Lectors should be chosen from among the most effective ones in your parish. It is an honor to serve in this ministry for the Easter Vigil and most, if asked, will participate. Make sure they have their assigned reading text well in advance, and any notes you can provide to assist them in prepara-tion. Consider a gathering early in Holy Week, or even on the Saturday before Palm Sunday, to listen to each other, offer critique, pray together, and review any logistics questions.

Tonight should see the best collaboration among your various parish music ministers that is possible. Adults and children, organists and guitar-ists, brass and timpani, handbells and violins: all have something to offer in music ministry tonight. Start preparing in January, not March. Consider carefully the balance of familiar music that the faithful will know by heart and the inclusion of once-a-year music that will require more leadership.

The most competent altar servers are needed tonight. Assign one as book-bearer: his or her only role is to accompany the presider wherever he goes, holding the "missal" for him. Assign two of them as candle-bearers, to as-sist with the sprinkling rite, and to assist during the preparation of the gifts. Finally one should serve as thurifer; incense will be used generously tonight. Gather them for a rehearsal early in Holy Week, and walk through every-thing they will need to do. Have them arrive at least forty-five minutes before the liturgy is to begin, so they can double-check things and not feel rushed in their preparation.

Hospitality ministers are needed in abundance tonight. Ideally, you have a large crowd of people to move from an outdoor blazing fire, in darkness, into a darkened church. Then, later on, from the nave to the baptistery. Worship aids and candles will need to be given out. There will be many visitors and guests of those to be initiated. Make sure all ushers and greeters understand the routes and timing of the processions.

The parish's initiation (RCIA) team should be fully engaged tonight, guiding the elect and their companions, families, and friends through this exciting liturgy. They should be rehearsed earlier in the week to assist at the font in the giving of candles, white garments, and so on.

As we discussed in chapter 2, the ministry of a vested master of ceremonies may be invaluable tonight. Choose someone who can fulfill this role with grace and skill, someone who is trusted by the preparation team and the presiding priest. Get him or her on board as early as possible, trust him or her to run the ministers' rehearsals, and guide this long and complicated liturgy effectively.

To safely and effectively build and sustain a blazing fire, recruit a team of people (perhaps the local Boy and Girl Scout troops) to handle this task.

To ritually decorate the altar during the Gloria (see below), invite as many people as you can manage to carry flowers, linens, candles, and so forth. Your art and environment team members, past neophytes, RCIA team members, or another parish group could perhaps fulfill this role.

Part 1: The *Lucernarium* (Service of Light)

Fire

The Roman Missal directs, "A blazing fire is prepared in a suitable place outside the church" (Easter Vigil in the Holy Night 8). This is not a pile of sticks, or a polite fire-starter log from the local grocery store. This is a fire whose light truly dispels the darkness of night. Make sure it is burning at least thirty, ideally sixty, minutes before the liturgy is to begin. Gather enough wood to sustain it that long. Build it far enough away from the church doors to allow the crowd to gather around it, but close enough that the procession into the church isn't overly long. Perhaps invite the local fire department to send some firefighters to supervise; they may even join in—that's evangelization!

 ART & ENVIRONMENT TIP: Note that the rubrics envision the fire lit before the people arrive; otherwise, the Missal would specify that the people gather around a "pile of sticks." The important lighting here is that of the paschal candle, not of the fire itself.

Make sure it can burn without active tending once the ministers arrive until after all have made their way into the church. A minister needs to have tongs to remove a burning coal, placing it inside the thurible, before the procession into the church.

Once the faithful have made their way into the church, the fire can be extinguished if necessary, or simply burn out if it can be done safely. The remains of the fire would be a wonderful visual for people arriving at the church in the morning, and perhaps pique the curiosity of many who have never been to an Easter Vigil.

 ART & ENVIRONMENT TIP: Many parishes have constructed a permanent fire pit for this once-a-year ritual. Once the ashes have cooled, spring flowers are planted in it for Eastertide. It remains a place for seasonal flowers and plants (not the social bonfires) throughout the whole year. Palms could be burned in it right before Lent, and it should be empty of all but ashes for the forty days.

Lights

Before everyone arrives, after the ministers are done preparing the church, all the lights should be put out: all of them. The night-lights that are always on. The overhead lights in the parking lot (the moon will be plenty bright). The LEDs on electronics should be taped over. Leave the fire exit sign lit for safety's sake, but that's it. Work with your facilities staff in the weeks prior to find all the circuit breakers you need to access.

Gathering

The people gather not in the church, but around the fire. A blazing warm fire and a pitch-black church will facilitate this actually happening. The contrasting symbols of light and darkness will speak more powerfully when they are utilized to their fullest potential.

Greeters should be welcoming people outside, handing them a worship aid and small candle, inviting them to simply mingle around the fire. There is no need to go inside. If the elderly or disabled who can't walk in procession need to wait inside, by all means escort them in. But warn them that at a certain time (ideally at least twenty minutes before Mass is to begin), it will be pitch-black in the church and other parts of the building.

There is no prelude music tonight, and ideally nothing needs to be rehearsed. Consider having someone welcome people and give them a brief overview of what is to happen. This welcome could remind people to turn off cell phones, explain how and when they will light their candles, and any other important details. In this modern era, you should also encourage people to simply follow the person in front of them as they walk in darkness; resist the urge to use the light of their cell phones to disrupt the powerful symbolic imagery that is characteristic of this night.

If the twenty minutes or so leading up to the liturgy start time feels like a festive bonfire on a camping trip—albeit a bit overdressed—you're probably doing it right. The weather, space, or safety concerns may require you to adjust your plans, but thorough preparation will allow you to use the powerful symbols of light and darkness to celebrate Jesus, the Light of the World, with great splendor this Easter Vigil.

Blessing of Fire and Preparation of the Candle

Once everyone has arrived at the fire outside, and the appointed time has come, the presiding priest, the deacon (or other minister) with the paschal candle, the thurifer and book-bearer, and other ministers go out to the fire. No one will need to announce his arrival: white albs and gold vestments will catch everyone's eye in the firelit night.

The presider greets the people in the usual way, with the sign of the cross and Pauline greeting, sung if possible. He then instructs the people about the Vigil using the words in the Roman Missal or similar ones.

 PRESIDING TIP: Choose these words carefully, in advance, to assist the faithful in understanding what will unfold and the importance of this night in the context of both the Triduum and the entire year. At no time tonight should even the most adept veteran presider be improvising his comments.

The blessing of the fire and preparation of the candle takes place as in the Missal. Note that elements of the candle preparation are optional, and can be done in advance. Consider carefully how much of the candle preparation can be done in the darkness, by a hot fire, with the pressure of the assembly looking on. It is possible to mark the candle in advance with Alpha and Omega and year, and simply trace those symbols while speaking the words. The incense grains should be carried to the fire and can easily be placed in the candle if the holes are predrilled properly.

Finally, the paschal candle is lit from the new fire. The presiding priest should do this using a bundle of tapers or an extension lighter—a small wax or wooden taper will be incinerated by the blazing fire.

One of the fire-tenders safely removes a burning coal from the fire, placing it in the thurible, into which incense is added by the presiding priest for the procession. To ensure success here, put a regular charcoal (preferably an easy-light one) in the thurible ahead of time, and let the embers from the fire light it. Both coals burning will produce plenty of fragrant smoke to fill the darkened church and lead the procession.

The Procession into the Church

The deacon (or other minister with the candle) then follows the thurifer toward the church. The presiding priest and other ministers follow, leading the rest of the assembly. The Missal describes where and when the procession stops. Consider if you can make these locations the same as where the cross stopped for an acclamation on Good Friday.

 PRESIDING TIP: Note a rubric in the latest edition of the Roman Missal that indicates the presiding priest lights his candle before the rest of the assembly. Most people will probably not notice this.

Other than candlelight and sung acclamations, the procession should take place in darkened silence.

All go to their places in the church, after lighting their candles, and remain standing. The deacon takes the paschal candle to its stand near the ambo.

The Missal indicates that after the third and final acclamation, the lights in the church are lit. It does not require that all lights be lit. It doesn't specify which lights should or could be lit. Consider keeping most of the lights out, at least during the *Exsultet*, which presumes the primary light is that of the paschal candle, not bulbs in the ceiling.

The Easter Proclamation (Exsultet)

The deacon then chants the Easter proclamation, an ancient element of the Easter Vigil. The *Exsultet* is sung by the deacon, assuming he can sing well. If he cannot sing well, a priest or cantor can sing it. The value is that this ancient solemn proclamation be sung well, by whomever can do so. Ideally, the only light used by the deacon is that of the paschal candle, as the proclamation indicates. If small battery-operated lights are needed, and can be hidden from view of the assembly, fine. Otherwise, memorization and familiarity will help this proclamation be rendered well. Place the *Exsultet* book on the deacon's chair before the liturgy begins, and he can carry it to the ambo similar to a typical gospel procession. For a lay cantor, place the musical notation on the ambo ahead of time.

After this, all are seated, extinguish their candles, and the presider introduces the Liturgy of the Word. This is a good time to bring most of the lights in the church up. While celebrating the Liturgy of the Word in darkness, perhaps restoring lights to full later during the Gloria or Alleluia might seem to preserve a nice "mood"; the dualistic symbolism of light and darkness belongs to the *Lucernarium*, which is now concluding. Also, darkness during the Old Testament that gives way to light during the New Testament may misrepresent the church's teaching about the value of the Hebrew Scriptures.

Part 2: The Liturgy of the Word

Readings, Psalms, Prayers

The reading of the word of God is a "fundamental" part of the Easter Vigil, according to the Roman Missal. The Missal specifies that all seven readings from the Old Testament, the epistle from Romans, and the gospel of the Resurrection should all be used, "whenever this can be done." I'm sure there are some situations in which this really can't be done, but those should be the exception rather than the rule.

If your parish has used less than the full complement of readings in the past, make a plan to restore the fullness of the Liturgy of the Word. Don't try to jump from only three Old Testament readings to all seven in one year—add one each year for a few years, and you'll have more success.

If, for "serious pastoral circumstances," you need to reduce the number of readings, you must read Exodus 14, and two other Old Testament readings, as well as the epistle and gospel.

A responsorial psalm is prescribed to follow each of the Old Testament readings. In some cases, there are options from which you can choose one psalm. It is also permitted to substitute a period of sacred silence after one or more of the readings, instead of singing the psalm. Following the psalm or sacred silence, the presiding priest leads a collect-style prayer, with everyone standing.

 PRESIDING TIP: For some of these prayers, there are multiple options from which you can choose. As you prepare the presider's text, choose the prayers that speak most powerfully to your community. Make sure to point them up for chanting, or make notes so the presiding priest can sing them well.

After the seven Old Testament readings, their accompanying psalms, and collect-style prayers have taken place, the Liturgy of the Word continues with the singing of the Gloria in Excelsis. Strange in its position this night, after some of the readings, its location is a holdover from an earlier liturgical era, where the vigil of readings was not considered part of Mass itself, but more a "prelude" to the actual Mass.

In his book *Glory in the Cross* (Liturgical Press, 2011), Paul Turner traces the postconciliar reforms of the Easter Vigil and explains how the Gloria retained its place in the modern Easter Vigil liturgy, between the Old and New Testaments. It fits, as in the biblical narrative, between the period of preparation for redemption and the beginning of redemption itself (*Glory in the Cross*, 141–42).

Gloria Procession

In the current order of things, the Gloria follows the Old Testament, and precedes the collect. During the singing, candles may be lit and bells rung (the first time since the Gloria on Holy Thursday). Some communities choose to use the Gloria as a moment to "dress up" the church for Easter. Honoring the rubric that the altar remains bare on Holy Saturday until during the Vigil, a procession takes place during the singing of the Gloria to make the church look like Easter.

The rubrics of the Missal direct that candles are lit at this time. Perhaps those lit candles could lead this procession, brought to the altar. Other candles could also adorn the sanctuary or other parts of the church, provided that they do not compete with the paschal candle, which should remain the only candle at the ambo. Flowers could be carried in procession and placed around the altar, ambo, and other appropriate spots in the church. A large white cloth and other vestments for the altar could also be brought and the altar be dressed at this time.

Recruit parishioners to take part in this procession, and rehearse them before the lights in church go out prior to Mass. Number each flowering plant on both the bottom of the pot and the floor where it should be placed, making for an easy procession and placement. Former neophytes, sponsors, RCIA team members, members of the parish art and environment team—all these make wonderful people to take part in this procession.

Work with the music ministry to ensure that there will be a long enough Gloria to ensure everything can be processed and placed. Make sure you rehearse this before Mass or at some other time, so it looks graceful and purposeful, not scattered and chaotic.

Following the Gloria, there is a collect, as in any other Mass, and then all are seated for the epistle from Romans. If the lights in the church and adjacent areas are not already fully lit, now's the time. If you turned off the parking lot lights before Mass, assign someone to turn them back on sometime between now and when people will head for their cars after Mass.

Alleluia and Gospel

Then, a once-a-year ritual takes place, restored to prominence in the most recent edition of the Roman Missal. The priest solemnly intones the Alleluia, after our forty-day fast from this chant. The rubrics direct that the priest intone Alleluia three times, raising the pitch by a step each time, with the people repeating it.

There is notation for this in the Missal itself, albeit a complicated setting. It could also be accomplished by the priest intoning the refrain of whatever gospel acclamation you will use this night, starting a few keys lower and working up to the key that the accompanied acclamation will be in. Ideally, the people respond to each of these three intonations by the priest. The Missal permits the psalmist to intone this if the priest is unable to do so well.

Psalm 118 is also proclaimed, with the response Alleluia.

MUSIC TIP: It is as if the responsorial psalm and gospel acclamation are combined into one musical element this night, preceded by a solemn intonation by the priest. Work with presiding priest and music ministers to ensure that this whole sequence of singing will be well rendered.

The Liturgy of the Word now reaches its high point—as it usually does—in the proclamation of the gospel. The deacon, ideally chanting at the ambo, proclaims the synoptic account of the year. Note that incense is used here, but no candles: the light of the paschal candle is enough. Since the gospel book was placed on the altar before Mass began, it can now be carried to the altar by the deacon, with incense, just like a typical gospel procession.

DEACON TIP: Make sure you clip chant notation for the gospel inside the book itself. If the setting of Psalm 118/gospel acclamation is lengthy, the deacon could go from chair to altar to ambo by an extended route, led by the thurifer. Because the music here is more developed than a typical gospel acclamation, make sure the deacon and thurifer know when and where to move.

Finally, the Liturgy of the Word concludes with a homily, which—even if brief—is not to be omitted. There is much to preach on this night.

PREACHING TIP: Resist the temptation to simply use an Easter Sunday morning homily tonight. While both liturgies celebrate the mystery of the Resurrection, they are different in scope, assembly, and ritual.

This homily need not be lengthy, but should be powerful and help the assembly understand Christ's presence in the many symbols, words, and sacraments that are celebrated this holy night.

Following the homily, the Liturgy of the Word is complete. The renewal of baptismal promises later on replaces the Creed, and the universal prayer takes place following the liturgy of initiation. A healthy period of silence following the homily may provide everyone a chance to catch their breath, to contemplate the powerful Liturgy of the Word, and a moment to transition into the next part of this multistage marathon!

Part 3: Baptismal Liturgy (Liturgy of Initiation)

This third part of the Easter Vigil is the most complicated. This is due partially to the fact that you need both the Roman Missal and the Rite of Christian Initiation of Adults together to understand the order of the rites. The sequence and combination of rites to be celebrated will be based on exactly who is to be initiated.

- Baptism of one or more unbaptized adults or children of catechetical age
- Baptism of one or more unbaptized adults or children of catechetical age *and* infant(s)
- Baptism of one or more unbaptized adults or children of catechetical age and the reception of non-Catholic Christians into the church
- No initiation whatsoever

The Easter Vigil has a long association with baptism, especially that of adults. In recent years, the RCIA has provided the option of also initiating baptized Christians who have not yet been confirmed or received First Communion. While this option remains legitimate, many liturgical scholars advocate strongly for the completed initiation of baptized Christians to take place at another time, during the Easter season or otherwise. The Easter Vigil should remain for the unbaptized. This, of course, is easy on paper, but complicated in practice. A baptized spouse of an unbaptized catechumen may wish to complete his initiation at this same liturgy in which his

wife will be fully initiated. Perhaps they have a young child who is unbaptized. Pastoral practice may suggest that all three be initiated at the Easter
Vigil, which is perfectly legitimate.

Work with the initiation ministers in your parish, ideally in January, and
certainly by Ash Wednesday, to determine who will be initiated at the coming Easter Vigil. Consult your diocesan office of worship or other chancery
office as to what the norms for initiation are in your local church. For more
information on this complicated issue, check out Paul Turner's *When Other
Christians Become Catholic* (Liturgical Press, 2007).

Ideally, the liturgy of initiation takes place in the baptistery if this can be
seen by the faithful. If space permits, there is no reason that the entire assembly (or at least young children who can't see well) couldn't leave their
pews and process to the font along with ministers and elect. If the font is
not visible to the assembly, nor room for all to gather in the baptistery, a
vessel of water can be placed in the sanctuary.

If there are candidates to be baptized, they are called forward and pre-
sented to the assembly by their godparents. A member of the initiation
team or the deacon or another suitable person invites those to be baptized
to come forward, by name, and stand before the assembly. If the godparents
will speak words of presentation of the elect, make sure they can be heard
using a microphone. If the elect are already well known to the community
(from the rite of acceptance, rite of sending to the bishop for election,
scrutinies, and communications media), no verbal introduction by the
godparents is necessary.

If there is a procession to the baptistery, a minister with the paschal candle
(preferably the deacon who carried it earlier) leads everyone while the
Litany of the Saints is sung. If no one is to be baptized, the litany is omitted
and the blessing of water takes place immediately. If there is no procession
to the baptistery, the litany is sung after a brief invitation by the presiding
priest.

Litany of the Saints

This ancient litany, found in the rites of baptism and ordination, implores
the cloud of faithful witnesses to intercede for those about to receive God's
sacramental grace. It accompanies the procession to the font. The sequence
of saints is specified in the Missal itself and other saints (the patron of the
church, the patrons of those to be baptized) may be added. There are additional invocations particular to this night. There are texts to be used if
there are people to be baptized and if there are not.

MUSIC TIP: The Missal specifies that two cantors lead this litany with the people responding, and all are standing because it's the Easter season. This is a lengthy musical element, which deserves much preparation and rehearsal. Either the chanted notation in the Missal or another musical setting may be used. Do not cut the litany short even if everyone has arrived at the font early; it's not simply "traveling music," but rather an important liturgical-musical element unto itself.

A brief prayer led by the presiding priest follows the litany and leads into the blessing of water.

Blessing of Baptismal Water

Even if no one will be baptized tonight, the font should be blessed for baptisms throughout the year, and the water will be used for sprinkling the people tonight and on Easter Sunday morning. Chant notation for the blessing of water is found in the Missal itself. If the presiding priest cannot sing it, it can be merely recited. If no one is to be baptized, there is a simpler version of the blessing in the Roman Missal (Easter Vigil in the Holy Night 54).

An ancient tradition remains as an option in the current edition of the Missal: toward the end of the blessing formula at the words of epiclesis, the priest can take the paschal candle and lower it into the water once or three times. Be careful that you do not ruin the candle or your fresh clean water by doing this (wax and water don't mix!), but consider carefully using this ancient symbolic ritual. It helps to mark the central prayer of this lengthy blessing formula, namely, the calling down of God's Spirit to make holy these waters and bring all who are baptized in them to new life in Christ.

 MUSIC TIP: The blessing of water concludes with a simple acclamation sung by the people: "Springs of water, bless the Lord; / praise and exalt him above all for ever" (Easter Vigil in the Holy Night 47). This will be unfamiliar to most, and seemingly come out of nowhere, so perhaps a cantor or the choir could sing it once and everyone repeat.

An important question to ask in preparing the liturgy of initiation is, how will baptism take place? Obviously, if your font is too small for immersion, baptism will take place by pouring water over the head. If the font is large enough for immersion—full or partial—you should embrace this possibility. It may be a scary proposition for some of the elect, but with some preparation and discussion about logistics, it will likely be possible. The church prefers baptism by immersion, as it does the fullest use of any sacramental sign, so work with your initiation team and elect to encourage this practice and facilitate its safe and comfortable execution.

 PRESIDING TIP: This question is important because if the elect will enter the font, the minister of baptism could do the same. The priest need not go under the water, but simply stand in it. If he removes his chasuble and shoes before leaving the chair, a wet hem of an alb and wet feet will dry easily enough.

If the minister of baptism will enter the font, there is no reason why he can't do so as the Litany of the Saints is concluding. He could lead the blessing of water and all other rites leading up to the sprinkling of the people with baptismal water while standing in the font, assuming the book-bearer can stand near enough outside the font to hold the book close enough. The deacon and other ministers can give the white garments and candles from outside the font while the presider speaks the text still in the font. Simply put: the presiding priest remains stationary in the font for most of this rite, and everyone else moves around him. This provides a focal point for both assembly and elect, and makes great use of the symbol of water. Consider this option, and practice the choreography and positioning of the rites at the font so everyone is comfortable with whatever you choose.

Renunciation of Sin and Profession of Faith

Like the rite of baptism celebrated on other days, either within or outside of Mass, the elect (or if infants, their parents and godparents) renounce sin and profess faith. Ideally, assuming there are only a few to be baptized, each person does this individually. Each enters the font, one by one, renounces sin, professes faith, and is baptized. If candidates do not enter the font, they can still speak these words individually. If there are a large number to be baptized, it's possible to have everyone renounce sin as a group, but the profession of faith ("Do you believe in God . . .") should be done individually, immediately before each is baptized.

Baptism

Then each candidate is baptized individually, ideally by partial or full immersion. The trinitarian formula is sung or spoken by the minister of baptism, to which all sing a brief acclamation, preferably Alleluia.

 MUSIC TIP: Consider using as a response the same acclamation setting used with the verses of Psalm 118 before the gospel.

If there are infants or children younger than catechetical age (generally about seven), they should be chrismated now. Adults and children older than seven will be fully confirmed later on tonight and don't need this anticipatory anointing from the rite of infant baptism.

All those baptized should be given a white garment and a candle lit from the paschal candle. Use the sequence of rites and texts found in the RCIA. The deacon and other ministers should assist in the giving of these symbols, and the godparents of the neophytes can assist them in receiving them. If immersion took place, have plenty of fluffy towels (white or ivory, no crazy patterns!) to help the neophytes stay warm and dry.

Now, the focus shifts from the neophytes to the entire assembly, who will renew the vows of their own baptism and be sprinkled with baptismal water. The rubrics of the RCIA and those in the Roman Missal don't match here. The Missal assumes that confirmation takes place before the renewal of baptismal promises, but the RCIA assumes that the assembly's renewal and sprinkling takes place before the anointing, which ideally takes place in the sanctuary. Ideally, the renewal of baptismal promises is led by the priest in the baptistery (perhaps still remaining in the font) and then the sprinkling with baptismal water takes place. At the conclusion of the sprinkling rite, the presiding priest and other ministers who assist him return the blessed water to the font, and return to the sanctuary.

If the neophytes have been immersed, they are still standing near the font, accompanied by their godparents holding a white garment and lit candle. Once the sprinkling rite gets underway, the neophytes could quickly exit the church, change out of wet clothes, and don their white garments. This is possible if the church is large and the sprinkling rite is lengthy. It's even more possible if there are baptized Christians to be received into the full communion of the church this night, which takes place following the renewal of baptismal promises, but before confirmation.

The neophytes should know in advance that there is no time for "hair and makeup"! All that is possible here is a quick trip to a changing room near the baptistery—prepared and marked in advance—to remove wet clothes and quickly put on their white garments. If, unfortunately, there is no time for the neophytes to change due to a quick sprinkling rite and no reception of candidates into full communion, they will have to dry off well with towels and their white garments can keep them warm.

Renewal of Baptismal Promises

Following the rite of baptism, the entire assembly is invited to renew their baptismal promises. Prior to this, the assembly relights their candles, used earlier in the Service of Light, from the paschal candle.

 DEACON TIP: In most cases, it will be impossible for all present to light their candles directly from the paschal candle. One possibility is for the deacon or other minister who has carried it to the baptistery to lower it, allowing several preassigned people (perhaps RCIA team members, ushers, anyone really) to light candles from it. They can then disperse throughout the church, helping everyone get their candles relit.

The priest could begin to introduce the ritual while the last of the assembly's candles are being relit. He then invites them to renounce sin and profess their faith. Following this exchange of dialogue, he then takes blessed water and sprinkles the people.

 MUSIC TIP: During the sprinkling rite, the chant *Vidi aquam* ("I saw water") or other text with a baptismal character is sung. Something with a simple refrain for the people, and plenty of verses to match the length of the sprinkling rite, will be helpful. Metrical hymns should be a last resort here.

If people have gathered in the baptistery, after being sprinkled, they return to their places in the nave. Once the priest and other ministers have finished blessing the people with water, they return the baptismal water to the font and process back to the chair. If all of the above has taken place in the sanctuary, the deacon now returns the blessed water to the font.

Whether the newly baptized have fully changed clothes, or have been waiting near the font, they take their place in the assembly at this point. All but the infants and children under age seven will be confirmed now, so rather than going to their place, they should simply go to the place where confirmation will occur (in front of the altar, steps of the sanctuary, etc.).

Reception of Baptized Adults
into Full Communion of the Church

If pastorally appropriate, baptized adult Christians can be received into the full communion of the church. As I noted above, there is a trend toward reserving the Easter Vigil for only the initiation of the unbaptized, and completing the initiation of baptized people on a different day. Any Sunday of the Easter season, including Ascension or Pentecost, would be appropriate days; really, a baptized person can be received into the full communion of the Catholic Church and receive First Communion nearly any day of the year. There is no reason, especially when candidates are well catechized and already immersed in the life of the Christian community, to delay the completion of their initiation.

Baptized adults who were not confirmed as adolescents should be confirmed at another time, preferably by the bishop. Infants can be baptized at the Easter Vigil, but, unless they are related to the elect or godparents, might appropriately be baptized at another time. (Most parents not already participating in this liturgy won't choose the Easter Vigil for infant baptism anyway.)

If you choose to receive baptized Christians into the full communion of the Catholic Church this night, that rite takes place now according to the RCIA. Just as you did for the elect, call them forward by name, with their sponsors, to stand before the assembly. Follow the rites and use the texts in the RCIA. Notice that the rubrics specify that those who will be immediately confirmed (which is presumably anyone being received this night) do not receive the laying on of hands.

If the newly baptized adults were immersed and needed to change clothes, you could delay their reentry among the assembly until after the rite of reception. This not only gives them more time to change clothes but also allows the focus to be on those to be received. After all have been received by the presiding priest, sing a suitable acclamation, during which the newly baptized can reenter the church with their godparents, taking their place alongside the newly received, in anticipation of confirmation.

 DEACON TIP: One way to choreograph this is to have two ministers (perhaps the deacons) lead the neophytes and godparents from the baptistery to the sanctuary during the acclamation following the rite of reception. The ministers could carry the paschal candle, which will now be returned to its stand near the ambo, and the sacred chrism, which will now be needed for the sacrament of confirmation.

Confirmation

The presiding priest will now confirm all those newly baptized adults and older children. While parents of older children not yet adolescent might ask to delay confirmation so as to be included later with their peers, canon law does not permit this. Children of catechetical age who are baptized must immediately be confirmed and receive Holy Communion, and the priest who will minister these sacraments needs no additional faculties to do so. A pastoral explanation for this is very simple: Because we believe that the sacraments are gifts of God's grace, why would we delay this gift when available now?

The rite of confirmation now takes place as found in the RCIA. Especially if there are multiple people to be confirmed, the ritual can be accompanied by singing. Once the confirmation is complete, the chrism can be returned to the ambry, or put away someplace convenient until after the liturgy.

 PRESIDING TIP: While it may seem tempting and appropriate to congratulate the newly initiated and officially welcome them, wait: they're not finished! Their initiation will culminate with the reception of Holy Communion, their first time at the table of the Lord. Save the round of applause for after the Communion rite.

The newly confirmed and their godparents/sponsors can either be seated now or remain standing in place for the universal prayer.

Universal Prayer

The liturgy of initiation comes to a conclusion with the universal prayer. Ritually, this takes place no differently from any other Mass. However, this is a special moment for the newly baptized, who will take part in this rite for the first time.

 PRESIDING TIP: Offering these prayers of intention is a right and responsibility of those baptized into Christ's priestly people, so a word or two of introduction by the presiding priest about this might be appropriate.

Even though there has been much singing already, singing the universal prayer might heighten the solemnity of this inaugural praying of it by the neophytes.

Following this lengthy liturgy of initiation, everyone is seated and the Liturgy of the Eucharist begins. If he took it off before going to the font, the presiding priest now dons the chasuble (if this is his first time returning to the chair) and sits down.

PRESIDING TIP: If the presiding priest has gotten wet during the liturgy of baptism, it would be possible for him to change at least his alb and stole in a nearby room to the chair, while the deacon(s) receive the gifts and begin preparing the altar. The priest can then simply don the chasuble, and go to the altar for the prayers of the preparation rite.

Part 4: Liturgy of the Eucharist

In all, the Liturgy of the Eucharist takes place like at any other Mass. If you don't typically have Communion under both kinds for all the faithful, consider doing so tonight, especially for the neophytes, godparents, sponsors, spouses, catechists, and others.

It is most appropriate that the neophytes (or if infants, their parents and godparents) serve as gift-bearers. Be careful that you don't ask them to come to the back of the church during the universal prayer, which they are taking part in for the first time. They can simply come back as everyone else is being seated at the conclusion of the prayer.

Along with bread and wine, you can bring the corporal and other fabrics to dress the altar, if not done during the Gloria.

If incense is being used tonight, lavish the altar, gifts, and cross with fragrant smoke. The presiding priest, concelebrants, and assembly should also be honored with incense on this night.

This is a night to sing part or all of the eucharistic prayer. If it doesn't seem appropriate to sing the entire prayer, consider singing the preface with its dialogue, as well as the epiclesis and institution narrative, in addition to the usual sung acclamations by the people.

The eucharistic prayer takes place in the usual way.

PRESIDING TIP: In Eucharistic Prayer I, there is a special mention and prayer intention for the newly baptized, which can be used tonight and throughout the entire Easter octave.

The Lord's Prayer and sign of peace take place as usual. The fraction of the bread also takes place as usual. Remember that there is nothing in the tabernacle, so no one needs to go there during the fraction rite.

Both the Roman Missal and the RCIA suggest that the presiding priest, before "Behold the Lamb of God," would give a little admonition to the neophytes. This admonition would be about the excellence of this great mystery, how Holy Communion is the culmination of their Christian initiation, and how the Eucharist is the center of Christian life. This should not be improvised; prepare a good, beautiful, concise text and include it in your binder/folder that is used throughout the liturgy. You can use the same text year after year. Of course, this admonition is heard by everyone, and serves as an annual reminder to us all of the importance of Holy Communion.

It could work well to have the neophytes come forward as the fraction rite is concluding, to stand nearer to the altar, perhaps at the base of the sanctuary steps. This would give prominence to this First Communion day and offer a focal point for the admonition.

The neophytes should receive Communion under both forms before others in the assembly enter the Communion procession. After the neophytes receive, Communion then takes place in the usual way.

MUSIC TIP: The Missal suggests singing the antiphon from 1 Corinthians 5:7-8 (a reading used on Easter Sunday morning) with verses of Psalm 118 sung earlier in the Liturgy of the Word. Any appropriate song can be used; one of your Communion processional pieces from Sunday liturgies, especially one imbued with texts of the paschal mystery, would be fine.

After all have received Communion, the remaining Precious Blood is consumed, and leftover consecrated hosts are reposed in the tabernacle, without any particular solemnity. Just do this like you do any other time. You can light the new vigil lamp after Mass has ended: everyone clearly sees that the Blessed Sacrament is once again reserved in the tabernacle.

There is a period of silence, like usual, and a post-Communion prayer. Any brief announcements could be made (ideally the routine ones can wait until next week!) including an invitation to a reception after Mass, and congratulations to the neophytes.

A solemn blessing is found with the other orations in the Missal, and could be used tonight. These are usually more effective when chanted, as the assembly knows better when to respond "Amen" to the chant tone.

The deacon (or in his absence, the priest) then dismisses the people using the formula with double-Alleluias as found in the Missal. The people respond in turn. This practice continues on Easter Sunday morning, and throughout the octave, returning again only on Pentecost.

There can be a concluding hymn, and the ministers can process in the usual way. The incense leads the procession, followed by the processional cross (used perhaps for the first time tonight) and candles. The neophytes and their families might be incorporated into the procession at the end, so they might easily greet everyone after Mass.

6

EASTER SUNDAY
OF THE LORD'S RESURRECTION

"This is the day that the Lord has made: let us be glad and rejoice!" The words of today's responsorial psalm (Ps 118) tell us everything we need to know about this holy day, the Sunday of Sundays.

Traditionally the most well-attended Sunday of the year, Easter Sunday remains an important feast day for Christians of every stripe. The good news of Jesus' rising from the dead, the paschal mystery, is the core of the Christian message. As we know, it is celebrated most fully during the Paschal Triduum. Unfortunately, many people's only entry into the Triduum celebration will be on Easter Sunday.

Since only a few special rituals mark the Easter Sunday Mass, it will be tempting to underprepare this liturgy, especially after the amount of energy, time, and attention given to the complex and unique liturgies of Thursday, Friday, and Saturday. Yet Easter Sunday morning deserves our focus as well, especially since for many, it will be *the* Triduum liturgy!

Art and Environment

The art and environment for Easter Sunday and the balance of Eastertide is established during the day on Holy Saturday, and crowned during the Gloria procession (see chap. 5). The only thing that might need to be done, if not already done after the Easter Vigil, is to fill holy water stoups using the freshly blessed water from the font. Otherwise, the church should be clean, bright, decorated in gold and white; chock-full of Easter lilies, colorful spring annuals, and green plants.

The paschal candle can remain near the ambo for Eastertide, or find another prominent place in the sanctuary for the great fifty days. It returns to its home in the baptistery only on Pentecost.

Your best altar linens and vestments should clothe the Lord's table, and you should use your best gold vestments on this day and throughout Eastertide. If you don't have a distinctive gold set for Eastertide, plan now for next year.

Introductory Rites and Liturgy of the Word

If you use incense only one Sunday a year, this is the one. It would be appropriate to incense the paschal candle, along with the altar and cross, during the entrance procession.

The presiding priest should sing the greetings and dialogues today, along with the orations (collect, prayer over the offerings, post-Communion). Since no musical notation is provided in the Missal for the three presidential prayers, make sure to point the text with marks, or insert some musical notation as needed into the Missal.

The Sundays of Eastertide are a privileged time to replace the act of penitence with the sprinkling rite. However, since today's liturgy includes the optional renewal of baptismal promises (see below), the sprinkling rite would follow that renewal. If you choose not to do the renewal, then the sprinkling rite would simply replace the act of penitence like any other Sunday.

This will be the first Sunday on which the Gloria is sung for a while. Choose a festive setting and dress it up with orchestral and rhythm instruments, handbells, choral descants, and so forth.

The first reading, like the other Sundays of Eastertide, is from the Acts of the Apostles. The psalm, like last night, is 118. You can choose between two different epistles, Corinthians and Colossians. Make sure preachers and lectors are on the same page (literally!) about which one will be proclaimed.

Sequence

Once a part of each Mass formulary, the sequence is retained in the Roman Rite for use only on a handful of days. It is obligatory on Easter Sunday and Pentecost Sunday. This poetic text functions as something of an extended gospel acclamation, sung after the second reading but before the gospel verse. It can be sung by choir or assembly or together. The Easter Sunday sequence *Victimae Paschali Laudes* is a beautiful ancient hymn extolling the Paschal Lamb slain for our salvation, Jesus Christ.

Decide who will sing what parts of the sequence, which envisions the assembly remaining seated. Make sure the thurifer and candle-bearers know that the gospel acclamation will begin after the sequence concludes—they should remain seated like the assembly before they bring the incense to the priest and candles to accompany the deacon.

Consider chanting the gospel on this day. Since John's account is used each year on Easter Sunday, it would be time well spent by the deacon (or priest) to learn it and render it well. The deacon should chant the greeting before the gospel, and the concluding dialogue as well.

Following the homily, either the Creed is recited or the renewal of baptismal promises takes place. Or perhaps baptism would be celebrated?

Initiation Today?

The Sundays of Easter are most certainly the ideal time for celebrating the sacraments of initiation. It is possible to baptize infants on Easter Sunday, but you should consider this carefully. Will the families of the infants be truly able to focus on this important moment or will they be consumed by family demands and holiday schedules? With capacity crowds and some already added rites, would extending Mass another several minutes be advisable or even possible? (Consider the parking lot.) For many people who attend Mass only infrequently, would the addition of infant baptism be evangelizing, or simply try their patience? Finally, with everything else that parish ministers have attended to over the past week, would adding one more thing be the best choice?

Unless you're not affected by the aforementioned factors, I'd suggest having infant baptisms on other Sundays during Eastertide. If you choose to baptize infants, the Creed is omitted, and the renewal of baptismal promises and sprinkling rite would take place following the rite of baptism, like at last night's Easter Vigil.

Renewal of Baptismal Promises and Sprinkling with Baptismal Water

The latest edition of the Roman Missal specifies that it would be appropriate to use the Apostles' Creed during Lent and Eastertide, because of its baptismal connection. Especially if you have done so during Lent and/or plan to do so during Eastertide, use the Apostles' Creed today. Nonetheless, you can certainly use the Nicene Creed as on other Sundays.

Or you can do the renewal of baptismal promises. Long an assumed part of the liturgy on Easter Sunday here in the United States, it appears now in the Missal as something of an option. In earlier editions of the Missal, the text itself appeared with the Mass formulary for Easter Sunday Mass during the day. In the present edition, there is simply a rubric permitting its usage and directing the priest to turn back in the Missal to the formulary for the Easter Vigil, since the text would be the same.

While there may be some situations where it would be pastorally desirable to simply recite the Creed as usual, I would strongly argue in favor of allowing the assembly to renew its baptismal promises on this feast of the Resurrection. Our baptism is the gateway to salvation because Christ has loosened the bonds of death. Unless we serve as a godparent or have our own infant baptized, we do not liturgically renew our baptismal promises but once a year, on Easter Sunday. Take this opportunity on the paschal feast day to allow the baptized to again renounce sin and profess their faith in God using the baptismal text.

If you have a font in the baptistery that is visible by the entire assembly, the priest, deacon, and other needed ministers should process to the font and lead the renewal from there. Make sure a minister brings the Roman Missal to the font, or have a spare copy there, or place a copy of renewal text in a folder easily carried or preset near the font. If you don't go to the baptistery, make sure a bowl of baptismal water from last night's Vigil is prepared in the sanctuary.

Just as at the Easter Vigil, but without lit candles, the priest leads the faithful in renewing the vows of their baptism. The people simply respond "I do." Following this sequence of creedal statements, the priest then sprinkles himself and the people with baptismal water. Like usual, an appropriate song with a baptismal character is sung. After all have received the water, it is returned to the font, or put away in a convenient place, and the priest returns to the chair.

The universal prayer then takes place in the usual way.

Liturgy of the Eucharist

There is nothing particularly unusual about the Liturgy of the Eucharist this day. Use your best vessels and linens, freshest bread, and choicest wine.

Use Preface I of Easter, with the text referring to "this day." Eucharistic Prayer I has a proper form of the *Communicantes* for this day. However, if you expect many "de-churched" people to return to Mass on this day, or you are affected by some of the issues I outlined above regarding baptism during Mass, you may be well served to use the briefer, more concise, and more easily comprehensible Eucharistic Prayer III instead.

This is a day to sing part or all of the eucharistic prayer. If it doesn't seem appropriate to sing the entire prayer, consider singing the preface with its dialogue, as well as the epiclesis and institution narrative, in addition to the usual sung acclamations by the people.

There is a solemn blessing formula with the texts of the Easter Vigil that can be used this day as well. Remember that singing this triplicate blessing will usually foster greater participation by the faithful than merely reciting it.

The deacon (or in his absence the priest) should dismiss the people with double Alleluias, and they will respond in kind. This greeting is used today, and every day until next Sunday, the octave day of Easter.

Hospitality

Since this day will see your church more full than most other Sundays, and many people will be unfamiliar with your building, hospitality is of utmost importance. As part of your preparation process, try to approach your church and this day's liturgy as a visitor or a non-Catholic or someone who hasn't been to Mass since Christmas. Would that person feel welcome and comfortable? What would that require?

Make sure there are enough well-prepared greeters and ushers to welcome people and get them seated efficiently. One suggestion is to augment your normal ministers of hospitality by inviting parish families who would normally attend the Mass to simply arrive thirty minutes early and serve as greeters. Families with young children will love to smile and hold the door, pass out worship aid booklets, show people to the restroom, and so on. If the weather is nice, make sure you have some greeters outside the door, so the spirit of welcome kicks in as early as possible!

Consider the cleanliness of your facilities. You've likely had many people come through your building since Thursday night. If your facilities staff (like most) is off on Good Friday and Holy Saturday, make sure that basic things are in order: full paper towel dispensers, extra toilet paper rolls, emptied trash cans, swept floors, dry floor mats if it's been rainy. All these things are important on any Sunday, but are even more important on Easter Sunday, and with a reduced staff may fall to someone else.

Worship aids are a near-must for this day. Even if most of the musical repertoire will come from a hymnal, an order of service will be most helpful for visitors and non-Catholics, as well as those who don't come to Mass weekly. They will struggle with some of the newly revised texts, and if you choose to use the Apostles' Creed, they'll certainly need that. A printed worship aid can include not only the order of service and musical elements but also words of greeting and liturgical catechesis. Make sure you have enough for the crowds you anticipate.

After the prelude music, consider a prepared call to worship or welcome statement read by a parish leader. This could be done by the pastor (if not presiding for Mass), a member of the staff, or any parishioner in a leadership role. Even if done by a lector or cantor, this verbal welcome could include some basic instructions, as well as some heartfelt sincere words of Easter greetings and welcome. Prepare this text and prepare the reader. Having this moment of transition between the prelude music and the entrance procession will not only help your assembly feel more at home but also allow the music ministers a chance to breathe. If the assembly has been noisy and loud up till now, this call to worship could include an invitation to a few moments of silence, which the liturgy always recommends before Mass begins.

Sunday of Sundays

I began chapter 1 talking about the primacy of the Paschal Triduum in the liturgical year. It's the prototypical celebration of the paschal mystery: it sets the tone for the entire liturgical year. In the same way, the Eucharist of Easter Sunday is the model for the other fifty-one Sundays. The fullest use of signs and symbols, the best efforts of all the liturgical ministers, well-crafted preaching, attention to hospitality—all these will help facilitate a prayerful, solemn, and beautiful celebration of the Paschal Eucharist. Not only will this inspire everyone who comes to pray on Easter Sunday, but it will set a tone for the remaining Sundays of Eastertide and, indeed, for the entire year that unfolds.

7

LITURGY OF THE HOURS AND OTHER PRAYER DURING THE TRIDUUM

We have looked in depth at preparing the principal liturgies of the Paschal Triduum, and there is much work to do. Yet the church gathers for prayer in other ways during these three sacred days, and these other liturgical and devotional services deserve our time and energy so they too are celebrated well and a source of blessings for the faithful.

Liturgy of the Hours

After the celebration of the sacraments, especially the Eucharist, the Liturgy of the Hours holds prominence in the church's liturgical life. In the daily prayer of Christians, time is sanctified and God is glorified. The Constitution on the Sacred Liturgy commends that the faithful should be encouraged to pray the Liturgy of the Hours in general; during the Paschal Triduum, many who would not ordinarily have time or inspiration might draw great strength from participating in the parish's communal praying of them.

The Liturgy of the Hours is the sequence of the church's daily prayer, focused on the singing of psalms. While there are several prayers marking various hours of the day, Morning and Evening Prayer are the principal hours to be prayed. Night Prayer also makes a fitting communal service, especially on Holy Thursday.

Evening Prayer (Vespers)

The rubrics of the Missal indicate that Vespers (Evening Prayer) is not prayed on Holy Thursday by those who participate in the Mass of the Lord's

Supper, nor on Good Friday by those who participate in the principal liturgy. Even those who participate in the Easter Vigil can pray Evening Prayer on Holy Saturday, but a communal celebration in the parish this evening may be difficult to organize. The principal church will likely already be well prepared for Eastertide, and the clergy and other pastoral ministers will likely be busy preparing for the great Vigil, which would begin in only a few hours. Nonetheless, perhaps someone could organize a communal praying of Holy Saturday Evening Prayer in a side chapel or other suitable space, and the faithful be invited.

Perhaps the most important communal celebration of Evening Prayer would take place on Easter Sunday. This evening liturgy officially concludes the three-day Paschal Triduum, which began on the evening of Holy Thursday. Sunday Vespers has long been commended as a wonderful addition to the parish's liturgical schedule; since this is the Sunday of Sundays, Easter would be a fitting time to celebrate.

Certainly, this will be a "tough sell" for the average parishioner, especially for those who have earnestly participated already in the principal Triduum liturgies, perhaps even returning Easter Sunday morning after a late night of paschal joy! No doubt those who would prepare and lead a communal liturgy like Easter Sunday Vespers are by now exhausted, and enjoying some well-deserved rest with their family and friends.

Yet the parish community could gather, no matter how few, for a celebration of paschal Vespers. In his wonderful book *The Three Days: Parish Prayer in the Paschal Triduum* (LTP, 1992), Gabe Huck outlines a simple service of Evening Prayer for Easter Sunday, following the ritual as found in the Liturgy of the Hours, and including the lit paschal candle, a procession to the font, and a water ritual recalling our baptism. Perhaps this would be a fitting time to regather the neophytes, their sponsors, and the initiation team, along with any other parishioners who would like to pray.

Morning Prayer (Lauds)

If your parish normally has Mass each morning, celebrating Morning Prayer (Lauds) on Thursday, Friday, and Saturday—all days on which a morning Mass is not permitted—would be a fitting way to encourage people to begin each of these holy days with prayer.

Use the psalms and antiphons, canticles and readings as found in the Liturgy of the Hours. Choose familiar settings to allow people to participate well. Prepare a worship aid booklet to assist everyone in participating, as most people are not familiar with the structure of this prayer form.

Holy Thursday Morning Prayer would logically take place in the church, but could also take place in a chapel or some other suitable space. If the Blessed Sacrament has been reserved after the Mass of the Lord's Supper in some place other than the main church, Good Friday Morning Prayer could take place there, in the presence of the Blessed Sacrament.

On Holy Saturday, it would be most appropriate to celebrate the preparatory rites with the elect as part of Morning Prayer. The RCIA describes these rites as taking place on Holy Saturday morning, and preparing the elect for what will take place later that day. They could include anointing with the oil of catechumens and the presentation of the Creed (if this has not taken place already).

Resist the urge to follow such a morning liturgy with the elect by a rehearsal of what will happen at the Easter Vigil. Allow this day to be one of contemplation and quiet prayer for those who will enter the saving waters during the great Vigil. Besides, no rehearsal is needed with the elect themselves. Rehearse the sponsors and initiation team members at some other time earlier in the week to preserve the stillness of Holy Saturday.

Night Prayer (Compline)

In addition to Morning and Evening Prayer, the Liturgy of the Hours includes Night Prayer. This simple prayer is typically prayed at the very conclusion of the day, before one retires to sleep. A logical communal gathering for Night Prayer could conclude the period of solemn adoration on Holy Thursday. Publicize that all are invited to close the first day of the Triduum with this communal prayer at the altar of repose. Provide a simple worship aid including musical settings for a hymn, antiphon, psalm, and Canticle of Simeon. If necessary, it could simply be recited, but you can likely find a cantor who could lead this simple liturgy unaccompanied.

If the only people in your parish who regularly pray the Liturgy of the Hours are the clergy and consecrated religious, it would be worth some time and attention to encourage this prayer by all the baptized. And there's no better time to start than with the Paschal Triduum.

Other Communal Prayer

Between the principal liturgies of the Triduum and some communal celebrations of the Liturgy of the Hours, there will be many opportunities for the faithful to gather together for prayer during these three holy days. However, make sure to allow for the faithful to gather for devotional prayer as well.

Traditionally, the Stations of the Cross are prayed on Good Friday. You could have an official communal celebration at some point during the day or in the evening. Be careful, though, to publicize this in a way that makes it clear that it is not a substitute for the principal liturgy, but rather complementary to it. If nothing else, ensure the church is open during the day for people to pray the Stations on their own.

While solemn adoration of the Blessed Sacrament concludes by midnight on Holy Thursday, there is nothing to preclude the faithful to pray before the reserved Sacrament throughout the night, until the Good Friday liturgy begins. And, as we noted in chapter 4, it would be laudable for the faithful to adore the cross following the celebration of the Lord's Passion throughout the afternoon and evening of Good Friday.

All of this, and other popular devotions, can nicely complement the principal liturgies of the Triduum, which should hold central place in your preparation process and publicity.

CONCLUSION

By now, you're more aware of the many details that must be mastered in preparing parish liturgies for the Paschal Triduum. Hopefully you've gained some fresh insights or been inspired anew by the beautiful texts found in the liturgy itself. Perhaps you're ready to rally the leaders in your parish to tackle this liturgical preparation with a new vigor. All these will lead to more fruitful, solemn, and life-giving liturgies for these three great days.

The parish that prepares for and celebrates well the liturgies of the Paschal Triduum knows that first things come first. Love is greater than obligation. Dying and rising is what it's all about. Praying well together during the three great days is our duty and our joy!

Appendix A
Palm Sunday:
Don't Overlook It!

Second only to Easter Sunday, Palm Sunday is usually the most crowded Sunday of the year in our churches. Many jokes are made about how people who don't normally come on Sundays will show up on days when they "get something" (palms or ashes), and that's one easy explanation. Yet I think there's something deeper going on. The liturgies of these four days in particular are the essence of the Christian mystery; they represent all that God has given us, all that God has done for us in Christ Jesus, and everything we are as children of God.

With its dramatic beginning, its bold liturgical color, its initial proclamation of the Passion, and its iconic Scripture proclamations, Palm Sunday of the Lord's Passion represents a significant stop on the Lenten journey. If a voice called out from the back seat, "Are we there yet?" our answer on Palm Sunday would be "Almost . . . almost but not quite."

Palm Sunday begins the final week of Lent, which the church has traditionally called Holy Week. It serves as something of a prelude to the Paschal Triduum, and therefore merits some attention in this book. While it would be a mistake to consider Palm Sunday to be "part of" the Triduum, it is helpful to see them as related, as we'll explore below. If nothing else, Palm Sunday of the Lord's Passion is an important Sunday among the fifty-two and therefore deserving of thorough preparation.

A checklist of important things to remember and prepare is found prior to those for the Triduum liturgies.

Art and Environment

The liturgical decor during Lent should remain for Palm Sunday, devoid of flowers, simple and austere. The violet decor of Lent could be accented by the red of Palm Sunday. Palms and olive branches could be added to the decor. Consider decorating the processional cross with palm branches to add festivity to the entrance procession. Use red vestments that are simple, and ideally different from those used on Pentecost or feasts of the martyrs. In all, make it clear that while Palm Sunday of the Lord's Passion is an important day in itself, it is also the Sixth Sunday of Lent.

Introductory Rites

The most distinctive element of the Palm Sunday Eucharist is its beginning, called "The Commemoration of the Lord's Entrance into Jerusalem."

The Roman Missal provides two different options for a festive beginning of Mass on Palm Sunday.

First, a procession can take place before the "principal Mass." This is mostly a holdover from earlier times in which only one "High Mass" was celebrated on Sunday in a parish. The rubric remains as a reminder that energy should be focused on one really great procession rather than going "halfway" at all the parish Sunday Masses. The procession originates at a smaller church or another suitable place other than inside the main church where the Eucharist will be celebrated. All the faithful are invited to participate in this procession.

If a procession can't take place at the "principal Mass," at the other Masses use the second option, a solemn entrance. This sees at least the ministers and possibly a representative group of the faithful gathering at a place outside but near the church, or even at the door of the church, to begin the liturgy.

In either case, the entrance antiphon "Hosanna to the Son of David . . . " is sung, the people are greeted by the priest in the usual way, palm branches are blessed and held by the faithful, and the gospel account of Jesus' entry in Jerusalem (from the synoptic author of the year, or even John in Year B) is proclaimed. Then there is a procession, while all sing antiphons along with Psalm 24, Psalm 47, or the hymn "All Glory, Laud and Honor." Once the procession reaches the church, the other introductory rites of the Mass are omitted and the collect of the day is prayed. Then, all sit for the Liturgy of the Word.

Finally, at any Masses where the solemn entrance isn't possible or pastorally desirable, the third option is a simple entrance. This basic option looks like the introductory rites of any other Sunday Mass, but includes a lengthy entrance antiphon, which if not sung, must be read by the priest. This option should really only be used for very small gatherings, such as in a nursing home or hospital, or other situation in which there really is no space for celebrating the introductory rites other than at the chair.

Liturgy of the Word

The first reading, responsorial psalm, and the second reading take place in the usual way. Use your Lenten gospel acclamation with the proper verse of the day.

The Passion is proclaimed today, as on Good Friday. Of the two, today's is secondary: in a way, it "anticipates" the proclamation on Good Friday. Today, we hear from the synoptic evangelist of the year, and on Good Friday, we always hear from John.

The Roman Missal is very clear about how the Passion is to be proclaimed and by whom. Chapter 4 on Good Friday provides some pastoral guidance on how to do this well, since the Passion takes place in the same way on both liturgical days.

Notice that a "brief homily" should take place, if appropriate. A period of silence may also be observed.

Liturgy of the Eucharist

Following the proclamation of the Passion, the liturgy of Palm Sunday takes place like any other Lenten Sunday. Use the same ritual music, observe the same ritual options, and so forth. To set the day apart from other Lenten Sundays, and to mark the entrance into Holy Week, consider departing in silence. After the post-Communion prayer, announce that the procession will take place in silence, and everyone is asked to depart in silence after the ministers have left the church. Reinforce this in a printed worship aid.

Hospitality

Perhaps above all else, make sure that hospitality is the order of business on Palm Sunday. Remember that many people who join you this day aren't here regularly. Perhaps they're even from out of town, or non-Catholic family members of your parishioners. Make sure your ministers of hospitality welcome everyone warmly, directing worshipers to coatrooms, restrooms, cry room, nursery, and so on.

Before Mass ends, don't forget to announce the Triduum schedule, or at least let people know where to find it. In this modern technological age, simply reminding people to check the parish website, Facebook, Twitter feed, or other platform will be just as effective as ticking off the schedule verbally at the end of Mass.

Appendix B
Timeline for Preparation

Right after the Triduum concludes:

✓ Make notes about what worked and what didn't—ask parishioners, ministers, ministry leaders, staff members. Get as much feedback as you can. You don't have to "fix" or "solve" everything; just note the problem and you can fix it next year.

At the first worship commission meeting after Easter:

✓ Use the evaluation tool found in appendix D to invite the commission to reflect upon their experience of the liturgy, especially in the areas of music, preaching, and art and environment.

January:

✓ The preparation team should review evaluation notes, watch video, review previous year's liturgies. Begin to think about any adjustments you'd like to make, or how to fix any issues from last year.

✓ Discuss any "big-picture" questions with preparation team, worship commission, ministry coordinators, and others, and make adjustments as needed.

✓ Finalize Palm Sunday/Triduum liturgy schedule, for inclusion in Lenten publicity and more immediate publicity as Lent is concluding.

Week before Ash Wednesday:

✓ Select and purchase new paschal candle.

✓ Order palms.

First and Second Weeks of Lent:

✓ Invite ministry coordinators to preselect any ministers, before making Triduum schedule openings available to all ministers.

✓ Recruit Passion readers for Palm Sunday and set a rehearsal/prep session with them.

✓ Update scripts for principal Triduum liturgies and invite others to review.

✓ Update ministers' notes for all Triduum liturgies and invite ministry coordinators to review.

✓ Prep art and environment team for Palm Sunday/Triduum decor, including timing and materials needed.

✓ Rally hospitality ministers for Palm Sunday/Triduum.

✓ Rally assistants for Holy Thursday footwashing (if needed).

✓ Prepare draft of Palm Sunday and Triduum worship aid booklets; confirm printing details with printer and/or office staff. Will there be one booklet for the entire Triduum, or separate ones for each day?

✓ Schedule any needed ministers' rehearsals (especially servers and Easter Vigil lectors) and put them on the parish calendar.

✓ Confirm Easter Vigil fire-builders.

✓ Recruit setup help for Holy Saturday.

✓ Schedule and prepare for RCIA sponsors/team Easter Vigil rehearsal late in Lent.

✓ Prepare Triduum full-parish email and postcard with communications staff.

✓ Confirm deacons' schedule for Triduum.

✓ Confirm presiding schedule for Triduum, including non-principal liturgies.

✓ Confirm preachers for principal liturgies.

✓ Confirm number of elect and order initiation candles to match paschal candle.

Third and Fourth Weeks of Lent:

✓ Confirm principal liturgy scripts and send to presiders and others.

✓ Confirm ministers' notes.

✓ Send finished worship aids to printer.

✓ Recruit liturgical ministers.

✓ Prepare footwashing assistants.

✓ Send lector notes for Palm Sunday by Friday before Fifth Sunday of Lent.

- ✓ Recruit people to help with parking issues for Palm Sunday Masses with outdoor procession.

- ✓ Check supply levels of bread and wine.

- ✓ Recruit someone to launder extra linens from Holy Thursday footwashing towels.

- ✓ Check on Easter Vigil assembly candles and purchase more if needed. Recruit some people to help assemble candles and drip-guards, or refresh them from last year.

- ✓ Confirm Holy Thursday food collection and who will make basket for gifts procession at Mass.

- ✓ Consider recruiting off-duty police officers to help direct traffic on Easter Sunday.

- ✓ Schedule meeting with head ushers for principal liturgies.

- ✓ Recruit parish leaders to read welcome statement/call to worship for Easter Sunday.

- ✓ If oils are to be carried in procession on Holy Thursday, recruit three oil-bearers.

Fifth Week of Lent:

- ✓ Meet with facilities staff regarding logistics details for Holy Week (e.g., automatic door schedules, security alarm time adjustments, Easter Vigil fire setup).

- ✓ Send ministers notes for Palm Sunday to all ministers (lector notes already sent).

- ✓ Meet with head ushers for principal liturgies.

- ✓ Walk through any particular details with presiders and deacons for Palm Sunday, especially changes from last year.

- ✓ Walk through any particular details with presiders and deacons for Triduum, especially changes from last year.

- ✓ Check for any critical gaps in liturgical ministry schedule.

- ✓ Confirm any concelebrants for Triduum liturgies and adjust extraordinary ministers of Holy Communion and seating arrangements as needed.

- ✓ Confirm website/telephone Palm Sunday/Triduum info with communications staff.

- ✓ Send ministers notes for Triduum to all ministers (or wait until early in Holy Week).

Holy Week:

- ✓ Print all texts, notes, and rosters and make binders.
- ✓ Carve new paschal candle, or ask someone to do so.
- ✓ Clean out oil vessels before Chrism Mass.
- ✓ Get new oils after Chrism Mass.
- ✓ Attend each day to the setup of each principal liturgy, as well as the liturgical "to-do" list for each day of the Triduum.
- ✓ After each liturgy, make evaluative notes for next year.

Easter Octave:

- ✓ Give thank-yous to everyone.
- ✓ Consolidate evaluative feedback into a document for review next year.

APPENDIX C
SETUP CHECKLISTS

Palm Sunday

✓ A copy of the introductory rites is in a red binder at the back of the church or at the place where the liturgy begins, so that the Missal itself need not be processed.

✓ Palms and any needed worship aids are available as the faithful arrive.

✓ Water and vessels for sprinkling are prepared.

✓ Additional Evangelaries or binders with the Passion text are placed appropriately.

✓ Candles and stands by the ambo have been removed. They are not carried at the gospel.

✓ For Masses with a procession, appropriate adjustments to the parking lot or walkways have been made. Recruit people in safety vests to ensure everyone can walk, drive, and process safely.

✓ The Evangelary is brought by the deacon and used for the processional gospel.

✓ If incense is to be used, the thurible is prepared in the usual way.

Holy Thursday
Issues to Consider Well in Advance:

✓ What publicity and catechesis need to be done in advance with the parish community? How will these be done and by whom?

✓ Is there a worship aid for the assembly tonight, or is it part of a larger booklet for the whole Triduum?

✓ What ministers not typically involved in a Sunday Eucharist are needed? Who will recruit them? Who will train them?

✓ Is a master of ceremonies needed? Who will it be and what will his or her duties be?

✓ What liturgical instruction and catechesis need to be given in the worship aid or verbally before Mass begins?

✓ Will a call to worship be given? By whom? If so, write one.

✓ What elements of the liturgy not normally sung (e.g., greetings, dialogues, orations, gospel) will be sung tonight? What musical notation is needed by whom and where?

✓ What texts other than those in the Missal and Lectionary need to be prepared? Who will prepare them?

✓ Will incense be used?

✓ If there are concelebrating priests, how will the eucharistic prayer be divided among them?

✓ If there are multiple deacons, how will the diaconal functions be divided?

✓ Will the oils/chrism be solemnly received by the community during this Mass? Who will present them and when? Where will they be displayed during Mass that night?

✓ What gifts for the poor will the faithful be asked to bring and how will they be incorporated into the liturgy?

✓ Who will be in the entrance procession and why?

✓ Will the church bells be rung during the Gloria and by whom?

✓ Will the *Mandatum* take place? Who will be involved and how? What preparation is needed?

✓ How much bread is needed for the Communion of the faithful for both Holy Thursday and Good Friday?

✓ Do we have a ciborium large enough to hold all the consecrated bread needed for Good Friday? If we use multiple ciboria, will they all fit in the tabernacle on the altar of repose?

✓ Where will the altar of repose be located? How will it be decorated? What is required for the procession and solemn adoration by the faithful?

✓ Who will strip the altar after Mass?

On the Day(s) before the Liturgy:

✓ The church is decorated with modest simplicity, clearly indicating that Lent is over, but Easter has yet to begin. NB: all flowers and decor will need to be removed after Mass concludes, before Good Friday.

✓ The Lectionary is prepared in the usual way on the ambo.

✓ The Evangelary is prepared to be carried in the procession by the deacon as usual; include chant notation if the gospel is to be sung.

✓ The Missal is marked and at the book-bearers chair as usual.

✓ Chairs are prepared for all ministers, including concelebrating priests.

✓ Prepared at the chair are any other texts as needed (act of penitence, universal prayer, musical notation, etc.).

✓ The tabernacle is empty with the door conspicuously open. The vigil candle is removed.

✓ The ambry is empty and the door conspicuously open.

✓ If they are included in the entrance procession, the oils (newly blessed/consecrated) are prepared in the designated place; a place is prepared in the sanctuary to receive them at the beginning of Mass.

✓ The font is completely emptied (including any other dependent stoups and fonts).

✓ The paschal candle stand is empty and placed near the empty font or in its usual place or removed entirely.

✓ The processional cross and candles are ready for the procession.

✓ The chairs, pitchers, bowls, and towels are prepared for the *Mandatum* ritual at the appropriate locations.

✓ The thurible, coals, boat, tongs, etc., are prepared in the usual way.

✓ The humeral veil is also at the credence table for use during the transfer of the Most Blessed Sacrament.

✓ The altar of repose is prepared with empty tabernacle, appropriate plants/flowers, candles, and linens. Adequate seating and kneelers are available. A kneeler is directly in front of the tabernacle so that the presider may incense the Blessed Sacrament while kneeling.

✓ If reposition takes place someplace other than the usual tabernacle, signs could indicate that the Blessed Sacrament is not reserved there.

✓ The usual vessels are prepared for Mass, including empty ciboria, which will be carried in procession at the end of Mass and used during the solemn adoration and subsequent reposition.

✓ The usual gifts are prepared in the back for the procession. Enough bread is prepared for the Communion of the faithful on Good Friday.

✓ Collection barrels could be near the doors to receive the people's gifts of food for the poor. Before Mass begins, someone gathers a representative sample of food into a basket, placing it in the back of church—this basket will be carried to the altar in procession along with bread and wine.

✓ The worship aids are at the doors or given out by ministers of hospitality. A worship aid is placed on the chair of the deacon and of minor ministers who will be carrying things in the procession.

Good Friday

✓ The altar is completely bare.

✓ The Lectionary is prepared in the usual way on the ambo.

✓ Gospel books or Passion books are preset from where they will be read or at another convenient place.

✓ The Missal is at the book-bearer's chair.

✓ If the chapel of repose was outside the main church, the usual tabernacle remains empty with the door conspicuously open. The vigil candle is removed and unlit.

✓ The font remains completely emptied (including any other dependent stoups and fonts).

✓ The paschal candle stand remains empty and placed near the empty font or in its usual place or removed entirely.

✓ A large cross is prepared for adoration by the faithful.

✓ Candles may be prepared in the back of the church for the processions of cross and Blessed Sacrament.

✓ At the credence table:
  ✓ Altar cloth
  ✓ Corporal
  ✓ Plates needed for distribution of Holy Communion
  ✓ (Lavabo, chalices, purificators, water cruet not needed)
  ✓ Humeral veil

✓ The worship aids are at the doors or given out by ministers of hospitality. Worship aids are placed on the chairs of all ministers who are in the procession.

✓ A basket for the collection for Churches of Central and Eastern Europe and signage are at the doors of the church.

Easter Vigil

✓ The Lectionary is prepared in the usual way on the ambo. The appropriate readings and page turns are marked for ease of the lectors' use with so many readings and options. A note is after the epistle that the Lectionary should be shelved as usual. The *Exsultet* book is preset on the appropriate deacon's chair or ambo.

✓ The Evangelary is marked and preset on the altar (if sung by deacon or priest)—it is not carried in the procession. Chant notation is included if the gospel is to be sung.

✓ A binder containing all needed texts from both the Roman Missal and the Rite of Christian Initiation of Adults, along with other needed texts (introductory comments, universal prayer, musical notation, etc.), is prepared to be used at the fire and carried by the book-bearer throughout the night.

✓ The tabernacle is empty with the door conspicuously open. A vigil candle is present, but unlit.

✓ An empty ciborium is near the tabernacle, for reserving any hosts left over from the Communion rite of this Mass.

✓ Candles are at the altar, but unlit. They are lit during the Gloria. Alternatively, these lit candles could be carried in procession during the Gloria, which may be easier than trying to light them during the singing.

✓ The paschal candle stand is empty and placed near the ambo (even if it will be elsewhere in the sanctuary for the remainder of the fifty days).

✓ At the baptistery:
  ✓ The font has been refilled and is prepared for the baptisms (towels, etc.).
  ✓ The ambry is open so the sacred chrism can be brought for confirmation.
  ✓ An initiation candle and white garment for each neophyte is prepared.
  ✓ An aspergillum or other implement for sprinkling the people is present.

✓ A changing room for the neophytes is prepared.

✓ If baptism is celebrated by full or partial immersion, a changing room for the presider is prepared, including dry vestments as needed.

✓ Appropriate pews are reserved for the elect, candidates, their godparents, sponsors, and families.

✓ The paschal candle is prepared for the procession. The bottom has been cut and will fit appropriately in the stand.

✓ The follower for the paschal candle is prepared where the candle is.

✓ Candles for the ministers, as well as a taper for lighting the paschal candle, are prepared. Make sure the taper used in the fire to light the paschal candle will withstand intense heat and light effectively. Bundling several long fireplace matches works well.

✓ The incense grains for marking the candle are also prepared.

✓ A fire is lit approximately thirty minutes before the liturgy is to begin. Wood is added as needed to keep it blazing until the liturgy begins. The fire needs to last at least until the procession goes into the church (approx. ten minutes after the liturgy begins).

✓ One of the ministers who prepares the fire has gloves and a tong, to retrieve coals from the fire to place in the thurible as the procession goes into the church.

✓ Worship aids and taper candles for all are prepared at the doors, and ministers of hospitality are distributing them.

✓ Extra candles for those who will help relight everyone's candles before the renewal of baptismal promises are located in a convenient place (probably in the baptistery).

✓ The thurible, coals, boat, tongs, etc., are prepared in the usual way. The thurifer brings the thurible and boat to the fire. A coal is in it unlit, even though one will be added from the fire.

✓ The usual vessels are prepared for Mass.

✓ Flowers, unlit candles, linens, and other decor items are in the back for procession to dress the sanctuary during the Gloria.

✓ The usual gifts are prepared in the back for the procession by the neophytes, perhaps including the corporal unless it is put on the altar during the Gloria.

✓ The processional cross is already in the church, for procession *only* at the end.

✓ As needed, small lights are prepared at the chair, ambo, cantor stand, piano, and anywhere else needed for the *Exsultet* and other parts of the liturgy done without full light in the church.

Appendix D
Evaluation Form

Theology

> "Since Christ accomplished his work of human redemption and of the perfect glorification of God principally through his Paschal Mystery, in which by dying he has destroyed our death, and by rising restored our life, the sacred Paschal Triduum of the Passion and Resurrection of the Lord shines forth as the high point of the entire liturgical year. Therefore the preeminence that Sunday has in the week, the Solemnity of Easter has in the liturgical year" (*Universal Norms on the Liturgical Year and the Calendar* 18).

✓ Did the Triduum as a whole suitably celebrate the paschal mystery? Was it truly the high point of our liturgical year? Consider specific examples.

✓ Was the Triduum clearly a distinct season from both Lent and Easter? How so or how not? Consider art and environment, preaching, music, devotional symbols and exercises, intercessions, variations in ritual.

✓ Did liturgical "variations" and liturgical choices (again: environment, music, preaching, other texts, devotional exercises/symbols, etc.) *reinforce* or *obscure* the reality that in each Eucharist "the victory and triumph of [Christ's] death are again made present" (Constitution on the Sacred Liturgy 6)? In other words, did the liturgies of the Triduum retain a fundamentally paschal character?

Art and Environment

> "During the liturgical year the Church unfolds the whole mystery of Christ, from his incarnation and birth through his passion, death, and resurrection to his ascension, the day of Pentecost, and the expectation of his coming in glory. In its celebration of these mysteries, the Church makes these sacred events present to the people of every age.
>
> "The tradition of decorating or not decorating the church for liturgical seasons and feasts heightens the awareness of the festive, solemn, or penitential nature of these seasons. . . .
>
> "Plans for seasonal decorations should include other areas besides the sanctuary. Decorations are intended to draw people to the true nature of the mystery being celebrated rather than being ends in themselves" (USCCB, *Built of Living Stones* 122–24).

✓ Did the Triduum accomplish this in terms of art and environment? Did the many significant symbols of the Triduum "speak" appropriately? Consider specifics.

✓ Did the altar, ambo, and cross retain their preeminence in the liturgical environment or did secondary and devotional items (cloths, candles, symbols, etc.) dominate?

Preaching

> "By means of the homily, the mysteries of the faith and the guiding principles of the Christian life are expounded from the sacred text during the course of the liturgical year" (Constitution on the Sacred Liturgy 52).

> "The very meaning and function of the homily is determined by its relation to the liturgical action of which it is a part. It flows from the Scriptures which are read at that liturgical celebration, or, more broadly, from the Scriptures which undergird its prayers and actions, and it enables the congregation to participate in the celebration with faith" (USCCB, *Fulfilled in Your Hearing* 42).

> "The preacher then has a formidable task: to speak from the Scriptures (those inspired documents of our tradition that hand down to us the way the first believers interpreted the world) to a gathered congregation in such a way that those assembled will be able to worship God in spirit and truth, and then go forth to love and serve the Lord" (ibid. 49).

✓ Did this happen during the Triduum? Consider specific themes, words, phrases, concepts, approaches, or styles.

Music

> "The Christian faithful who come together as one in expectation of the Lord's coming are instructed by the Apostle Paul to sing together Psalms, hymns, and spiritual canticles (cf. Col 3:16). . . . Great importance should therefore be attached to the use of singing in the celebration of the Mass" (*General Instruction of the Roman Missal* 39–40).
>
> "Among the many signs and symbols used by the Church to celebrate its faith, music is of preeminent importance. As sacred song united to words it forms a necessary or integral part of the solemn liturgy. Yet the function of music is ministerial: it must serve and never dominate. Music should assist the assembled believers to express and share the gift of faith that is within them and to nourish and strengthen their interior commitment of faith. It should heighten the texts so that they speak more fully and more effectively. The quality of joy and enthusiasm which music adds to community worship cannot be gained in any other way. It imparts a sense of unity to the congregation and sets the appropriate tone for a particular celebration" (Bishops' Committee on the Liturgy, *Music in Catholic Worship* 23).

✓ Did music "do its job" in the liturgies of the Triduum? Consider assembly singing, responsorial psalmody, choral/ensemble singing, presidential and diaconal singing/chanting.

✓ Was the liturgical music truly ministerial? Did it help the assembly express and share their faith? Did it heighten the texts?

Appendix E
Sample Texts

Easter Vigil Call to Worship

To be done by a pastoral minister, preferably not the presider or deacon, or other vested minister outside at the fire, approximately ten minutes prior to the liturgy's start time. The fire is blazing, the lights in the church have been put out, and people have gathered around the fire.

Welcome, good evening [etc.]

We gather this evening around the fire—just as people have done for ages unending.

We gather in darkness because we celebrate Jesus, the Light of the World, who destroys the darkness of death.

We gather just before the first Sunday after the first full moon after the first day of spring—the *sun* is ready, the *moon* is ready, the *earth* is ready, and so are we!

You should have received a candle and worship aid booklet as you arrived; if not, ministers are moving about to make sure you have one.

Our liturgy begins with the blessing of this fire, and the blessing and lighting of our new paschal candle, which will lead us through the darkened night into the church.

Once inside, the deacon will pause and you can light your candles from the paschal candle, or from one another, and then make your way to a seat.

Please just follow the person in front of you; you won't need anything but the light of the moon and of the paschal candle to see your way into church.

While in the procession, we also ask you to observe a reverent silence, as we process through the dark of night.

Later on in the liturgy, we will ask God's blessing upon the waters of our font, freshly refilled! No need to stop in procession at our unblessed font!

Finally, I invite you to simply take in the many sights, sounds, smells, and even tastes of this glorious night! We will begin shortly.

If there's time, the ministers then wait until the appointed time to come out to the fire.

Exhortation to the Neophytes before First Communion (Easter Vigil)

The Communion rite takes place in the usual way except as follows.

According to RCIA 594, before saying "Behold the Lamb of God" the celebrant may briefly remind the neophytes of the preeminence of the Eucharist, which is the climax of their initiation and the center of the whole Christian life.

He first invites them forward in these or similar words:

Presider: I now invite those who will receive Communion for the first time to come forward.

After allowing time for this to happen, he continues in these or similar words:

My dear friends in the risen Christ,
newly initiated into his Body, the church:
tonight you join us at the table of the Lord for the first time.

Your initiation into the Christian community will be complete . . .
yet your journey of discipleship has just begun.

The Eucharist is truly the source and summit of the Christian life;
through our sharing in this sacrificial meal,
we are privileged to participate in God's own divine life.

The Eucharist is a great gift, but comes with great responsibility:
that is, to proclaim the good news of the Resurrection
in all that you do and say.

He continues as usual:

Behold the Lamb of God. . . .

Annotated Bibliography

Ritual Books

The Roman Missal
This is your primary ritual book, containing the presidential texts and rubrics for the liturgies, as well as some introductory material (*praenotanda*) describing the liturgy.

Lectionary for Mass
This contains the readings and psalmody for the liturgies.

Rite of Christian Initiation of Adults
Use this book for all the liturgies of Christian initiation throughout the year, but especially the rites of initiation at the Easter Vigil. You'll need to use it and the Roman Missal together, as the books depend on one another.

Official Liturgical Documents

Universal Norms on the Liturgical Year and the Calendar
This Roman document governs the liturgical year and the organization of the calendar, situating the Paschal Triduum at the top of the hierarchy of liturgical days.

Paschalis Sollemnitatis
This "circular letter" released by the Vatican's Congregation for Divine Worship and the Sacraments offers practical guidance in observing the rubrics in the Missal. Issued in 1988, it was written in response to the implementation of the 1955 Holy Week reforms, in hopes of correcting missteps, and encouraging good liturgical practice going forward.

Other Books

Glory in the Cross: Holy Week in the Third Edition of The Roman Missal. **Paul Turner. Collegeville, MN: Liturgical Press, 2011.**
This book looks carefully at the rubrics and prayers of Palm Sunday, the chrism Mass, and the Paschal Triduum, commenting on liturgical history and development, especially noting changes found in the third edition of the Missal.

The Three Days: A Liturgical Guide. **Second Edition. Lawrence Johnson. Washington, DC: Federation of Diocesan Liturgical Commissions, 2012.**
This publication includes many of the source texts themselves, along with history, some underlying theology, questions for a preparation team's discussion, and more.

The Origins of Feasts, Fasts, and Seasons in Early Christianity. **Paul F. Bradshaw and Maxwell E. Johnson. Collegeville, MN: Liturgical Press, 2011.**
Bradshaw and Johnson lead us through liturgical history and trace the development of the various seasons and feasts, including *Pascha* and the Paschal Triduum.

Advent to Pentecost: Comparing the Seasons in the Ordinary and Extraordinary Forms of the Roman Rite. **Patrick Regan. Collegeville, MN: Liturgical Press, 2012.**
A definitive work on the development of the liturgical year including the history of the Paschal Triduum.

The Three Days: Parish Prayer in the Paschal Triduum. **Revised Edition. Gabe Huck. Chicago, IL: Liturgy Training Publications, 1992.**
Read this book for theological reflection and creative thinking about the liturgies of the Paschal Triduum.

Washing Feet: Imitating the Example of Jesus in the Liturgy Today. **Thomas O'Loughlin. Collegeville, MN: Liturgical Press, 2015.**
A wonderful reflection upon the Christian ritual of footwashing with some practical advice on how to celebrate the *Mandatum* well.

Lightning Source UK Ltd.
Milton Keynes UK
UKOW04f1521120117

291945UK00006B/194/P